# THE MOON OF THE MIND RISES IN EMPTY SPACE

LECTURES ON THE IL-WON-SANG VOW

# THE MOON OF THE MIND RISES IN EMPTY SPACE

Prime Dharma Master Kyongsan

Seoul Selection

# THE MOON OF THE MIND RISES IN EMPTY SPACE
Lectures on the Il-Won-Sang Vow

Published by Seoul Selection
105-2 Sagan-dong, Jongno-gu, Seoul, Korea
Phone: 82-2-734-9567, Fax: 82-2-734-9562
Email: publisher@seoulselection.com
www.seoulselection.com

ISBN: 978-89-91913-80-6   93220
Printed in the Republic of Korea

The original Korean edition of this book was first published in 2003
by Wonbook.

# Contents

Preface     7

The Il-Won-Sang Vow     14
Commentary on the Theme of the Il-Won-Sang Vow     16


**PART I**

## THE TRUTH OF IL-WON-SANG     29

Chapter 1 General Content of the Il-Won-Sang Truth     32
Chapter 2 The Il-Won-Sang Truth Is the Root of All Things     43
Chapter 3 The Changing and Immutable Creative     54
          Transformations of the Il-Won-Sang Truth


**PART II**

## THE PRACTICE OF IL-WON-SANG     95

Chapter 4 A Life Modeled Wholeheartedly on the Il-Won-Sang Truth     98
Chapter 5 The Life of Becoming a Buddha through the Threefold Study     114
Chapter 6 The Life of Progression and Grace     148
Chapter 7 The Result of Completing Our Vow     164
Chapter 8 Conclusion of the Il-Won-Sang Vow     176


Afterword     180

**NOTE**

This book used the Revised Romanization system for Korean words appearing in the text. In the case of certain terms and names related to *Won*-Buddhism, however, it followed the McCune-Reischauer system adopted in the English-language versions of the *Won*-Buddhism scriptures.

# Leading the Way to Building Il-Won World

In the *Analects*, Confucius says, "The business of laying on colors comes after the surface has been cleaned." This means we can only paint a picture once we have cleaned the canvas. When we cook rice, we first clean the bowl, and then we wash the grains. We clean our home before welcoming a guest inside, and we wash our hands before preparing food. In the same way, it is important that we empty our mind or "clean" it before we use it.

No matter how hard the rain beats down, the beads of water roll off the lotus leaf. If we can simply recover our clean original mind, the sensory conditions will roll away much as the rain trickles away from the lotus leaf, and our original mind will be restored. Similarly, before starting something new, we must first put our minds in order—only beginning once a clean and pure mind has been established. In organizing this lecture on the Il-Won-Sang Vow, I also cleansed my mind before beginning preparations, committing myself fully to establishing a wholesome heart before starting. If all of you hearing this lecture approach it having first established a clean and whole mind, the virtues of listening will be far greater.

\* \* \*

The history of humankind has seen many events that call for celebration. It was a great event when Benjamin Franklin discovered electric power, and it was great cause for celebration when the First and Second World Wars came to an end. In addition, the day the Berlin Wall fell in Germany, the day Yuri Gagarin traveled outside the Earth's atmosphere on the world's first space voyage, and the day Neil Armstrong set foot on the moon were all great events in human history.

But other events have occurred that were even greater than all of these celebrated events of external culture and civilization.

They came when great sages appeared in human history, like the rising sun and moon. When the Buddha came to this world three thousand years ago it was a truly great event, as was the arrival of Confucius and Jesus Christ.

The greatest event in all of human history came in 1916 C.E., the first year of the *Won*-Buddhist Era, when the Founding Master Sot'aesan achieved great enlightenment. The world is simply unaware of this. Once we open our eyes to the truth, we will see that the Founding Master's arrival on this Earth is cause for my celebration, for the country's celebration, for the whole world's celebration. If we do not feel that joy, it is because we have not yet developed the wisdom to know the truth.

When sages came to this world in the past, historical circumstances were such that the impact of the event was limited to their home region. The arrival of Confucius was a great event principally for China, the arrival of Jesus Christ for Judea, and the arrival of the Buddha for India.

Thus the teachers of the past were individuals who took

responsibility for one of the cardinal directions. Of course, these three sages are certain to have a great impact on spiritual civilization in the future as they have had until today. But the Founding Master came into this world as a teacher for all directions—north, south, east, and west—in a globalized era such as today. It is therefore an even greater event, and it is simply unfortunate that some of us have not yet experienced this event and awakened to its holiness.

In the past, it was a great event simply for a sage to have been born. Because of this, we have adopted the birthdays of these sages as occasions for celebration. The Founding Master, however, placed greater value on the day of his enlightenment than on the day of his birth. Whereas we emphasized the importance of births in the past because it was an age of fortune, we live today in an age of human rights, and so we place greater value on what enlightenment a sage experienced and what he did before departing this Earth.

Thus it is a fact of great significance that *Won*-Buddhism

regards the day of the Founding Master's great enlightenment as a day of celebration. In the future, external conditions will be of no importance: what family a person was born into, whether that person is a man or woman, what race that person belongs to, on what date that person was born. Instead, it will be a time in which we attach importance to the truth that one awakened to while living in this world, and what works a person has done, and judge the person on that basis.

*Won*-Buddhists should use these lectures on the Il-Won-Sang Vow as a way of gaining realization about their minds, of awakening to the truth of the universe, and of understanding the sort of things they should be doing while they are living in this world.

\* \* \*

Why did the Founding Master come into this world? He did not come to tell us, "Believe in my law." Rather, he came to make sages of all of us who live in this world.

During the March 1st Movement for Korean Independence,

the Founding Master heard the calls of students asking him to take part in the campaign. He called this a "funeral chant demanding a Great Opening." With the work of sharing the Great Opening under way, he went to Mt. Byeonsan and created the teachings. "One must not stop at catching fish with a pole," he said. "One must weave a net."

When he began the work of creating a doctrine and a plan, the Founding Master said that while the March 1st Movement and its goal of saving the Korean people were important things, it was even more urgent to provide something that could revive a morality suited to the future world, something that could save both the Korean people and humanity as a whole.

We now find ourselves ensnared in the net crafted by the Founding Master. It is a net that pulls us toward a paradisial world—the Il-Won world. Now that we are caught, we should not seek to extricate ourselves. Rather, we should allow ourselves to be taken where it leads, building a paradisial world, remaining with this dharma throughout numerous lifetimes, and changing the nameplate above our door. When our descendants write their genealogies, they will describe us not as "unenlightened being So-and-So," but as "sage So-and-So"—someone possessing the status of dharma strong and Māra defeated, the status of beyond the household, the status of tathāgata.

We live our lives without knowledge either of this world or the world that is to come. We have no birth and death insurance card to prepare us for the possibility of misfortune striking us at some point. We must therefore change our nameplate so that it reads "sage." I pray that you will study the Il-Won-Sang Vow so that you, too, can change your nameplate to that of "sage" and play a major role in the building of the Il-Won world.

# THE IL-WON-SANG VOW

"Il~Won is the realm of samādhi beyond all words and
speech, the gateway of birth and death that transcends
being and nonbeing, the original source of heaven and
earth, parents, fellow beings, and laws, and the nature
of all buddhas, enlightened masters, ordinary humans,
and sentient beings. It can form both the permanent
and the impermanent: viewed as the permanent, it has
unfolded into an infinite world that is ever abiding and
unextinguished, just as it is and spontaneous; viewed as
the impermanent, it has unfolded into an infinite world,
now as progression, now as regression, here as grace
arising from harm, there as harm arising from grace,
by effecting transformations through the formation,

subsistence, decay, and emptiness of the universe, the birth, old age, sickness, and death of all things, and the six destinies in accordance with the mental and bodily functions of the four types of birth. Therefore, modeling ourselves wholeheartedly on this Il-Won-Sang, the Dharmakāya Buddha, and practicing with utmost devotion to keep our mind and body perfectly, to know human affairs and universal principles perfectly, and to use of mind and body perfectly, we deluded beings make this vow so that, by progressing rather than regressing and receiving grace rather than harm, we may attain the awesome power of Il-Won and be unified with the substance and nature of Il-Won."

# Commentary on the Theme of the Il-Won-Sang Vow

### The Vow to Embody the Truth

The Il-Won-Sang Vow is a prayer that the practitioner offers before the Fourfold Grace of the Dharmakāya Buddha. It is a pledge to receive forever limitless grace from the utterly impartial and selfless power of the Il-Won-Sang Truth, and to become a great sage who attains buddhahood and delivers sentient beings by building the ultimate bliss of the self-nature through unification with the perfect and complete substance and nature of the Il-Won-Sang Truth.

Master Taesan described the Il-Won-Sang Vow as a pledge offered before one's mind-buddha. He said that it was a vow to our mind-buddha that we will live our life like the truth. Also, because the vow is designed to be recited out loud, it has the character of an invocation or prayer. In order to study the vow, we will first need to consider our own vows.

There are different ways of living one's life. Some of us live haphazardly, following whichever way the wind blows, and some live diligently, setting goals and working hard to achieve them. Those who lack goals simply expend their energies without rhyme or reason and without value before they depart.

Those who have a goal in life, however, focus their physical and mental energies on achieving that goal and are thereby able to live successful lives. If we look at those who have succeeded in this world, we will see that all of them are people who have led goal-oriented lives. Now we must also give deep consideration to what the goal of life is and to what we have vowed.

When we have a goal, we develop an interest in it, and when we develop an interest in something, we naturally come to develop an understanding of it. When we have gained an understanding, we can put it into practice, and once this has taken place, we are able to obtain something. However, the person who lacks a goal and a vow is destined to try just once, and then, when it does not work out, either to quit outright or to go back and forth, ultimately living a wavering life.

We must discover what it is that we truly want to do. If we are going to do that, however, it is more valuable and meaningful when our goal is to embody the truth, rather than worldly matters such as money, honors, or power. When we pursue worldly goals, even success may actually leave us experiencing greater troubles.

One cold and snowy winter day back when I was Executive Director of the Seoul Regional, I was on a train to Iksan sitting next to an old, elegantly dressed gentleman. So graceful was the snow that it would have been easy to succumb to sentimentalism, but as I talked with this old gentleman about various life matters, I came to hear about his discontentments.

"The people in this world call me a successful man," he said. But he confessed to feeling terribly lonely. He was the president of a small company, and in the process of passing the reins of the company on to his youngest son. His oldest son was a doctor. The old gentleman was quite boastful of his children.

He had earned his share of money and honors, yet as he found himself arriving at the end of life he realized that he could not avoid the thing called death. He was now set to depart, leaving behind all that he had worked so hard to earn. He said that all he could think about was that life is empty. He had come to keenly sense that life, as the lyrics of a popular song put it, is a "traveler's road."

He was a successful man, but what he ultimately shows us is that worldly success cannot enrich our souls. It is time for us to give deep consideration to the kind of goals that we have right now, and what it is that we are working so hard to possess.


### Toward the Life of Seeking to Possess the Truth

The vow to embody the truth gives us the power to escape the suffering of samsara, to possess truth, to possess the true self, and to use our mind and body as we wish. So we must go about making the new goal of our life the vow to embody the truth, and we must commit all of our energies to strengthening that vow.

Each of us must earnestly ask: What is my vow? Once that vow has been established, we need no encouragement to practice with fire in our eyes. Such is the importance of making this vow.

The meaning of the Il-Won-Sang Vow is that of a declaration that we will live our life like the Il-Won-Sang. The Il-Won-Sang means nothing other than the truth. In Christianity, the synonym for "truth" was given the name God; in Buddhism, the Dharmakāya Buddha; in Daoism, nature; in Confucianism, *wuji*. The Founding Master Sot'aesan called it by the name of Il-Won-Sang.

With the Il-Won-Sang Vow, the Founding Master took an interest in the lives of us ordinary humans and sentient beings, exhorting us to live our lives according to a vow that we have made. It is a prayer that he crafted himself so that each of us might possess the Il-Won-Sang Truth as our own and hold it in the palm of our hand.

For this reason, we must recite the vow over and over. Sometimes, we will need to read it reverentially, relishing and pondering every nuance of the dharma instruction. If we recite the text of the vow over and over—so that it pierces our brain and heart, our hands and feet—the spirit of the Founding Master's vow will suffuse our mind and body.

## What Kind of World Are We Building?

What kind of world have we built over the course of our lives, both past and present?

First, we have been building a world of hatred and love. Ordinary people spend their years loving and hating before meeting their death. What is it that we love so intensely and hate so intensely in our lives? These years of hatred and love are the life of the ordinary human.

Second, we have been building a world of ignorance for the sake of the flesh—living as we will, eating delicious things, grooming ourselves to look attractive, and giving ourselves over to pleasure. This is the life that we live as sentient beings.

Third, we have spent our lives cultivating all manner of pretensions in order to impress others. We have lived with the desire merely to look good to others and hear nice things about ourselves, rather than doing well by our selves. Ultimately, we have abandoned the true self and lived lives oriented toward others, and what we have accumulated as a result is nothing more than a vain sense of glory or false consciousness. This is the life of ordinary people.

Fourth, we have lived a life of objectification, banding together with others to slander and hate one another. Our livelihoods are not our own, for we are motivated by the thought that "I must do something now that my friend is a manager" or "I must do something now that my friend has succeeded and is making money." We have varied the course of our lives according to the success or failure, the fortune or misfortune, of the people whom we encounter.

We must not live the life of the ordinary person. We must change. The life of the ordinary person is an endless sequence of hatreds and loves, of living without rhyme or reason, and possessing no understanding of where we came from or where we are going.

My hope is that this lecture will motivate you to make a wish for yourself, so that your life will go from that of the ordinary human—a life of hating and loving and living blindly—to that of a buddha.

## What Do We Need to Possess?

The Founding Master believed that the greatest and most holy life was the life of possessing the truth, a life that ensures eternal life. It is for this reason that he gave us the Il-Won-Sang Vow—so that we might live lives of possessing the truth and building a world of truth.

If we trust the Il-Won-Sang Vow, awaken to the Il-Won-Sang Vow, and put the Il-Won-Sang Vow into practice, we can live a life of complete blessing and wisdom. Were he alive today, the

Founding Master would be praying even now that the road open wide ahead of the person who recites this vow, believes in it, and puts it into practice.

When a novelist publishes a book, he hopes that many people will buy it, read it, and enjoy it. The poet, too, hopes that many people will read his works.

In the same way, the Founding Master, in giving us this vow, would have hoped and prayed that many people would read, recite, and practice the sutra, so that they might avoid falling onto the evil path, gain the awesome power of the truth, and unite with the truth's substance and nature. The Founding Master's students, and all of the sages, heavenly beings, and asuras would pray that we fervently recite this dharma instruction from the Founding Master, the Il-Won-Sang Vow, and would pray that we believe in it, understand it, practice it, and commend it to others.

When we practice this vow, our life becomes one shared with the Founding Master, and with all the buddha-bodhisattvas of the three time periods of past, present, and future.

## The Words of Past Sages

The scriptures presented to us by the sages of the past have lost their luster over time. It is not that they are bad; rather, they have faded over the long years and become unsuited to the times. In the

*Diamond Sutra*, the Buddha spoke of the Final Age of the Law, the Saddharma-vipralopa. Jesus said that when the end came, he would come "as a thief in the night." This meant that when the end times came, he would quietly do what was entrusted to him and depart.

If we travel to Beopjusa Temple on Mt. Songnisan, we will see that the Buddha has been enshrined not on the inside, but on the outside. This is, presumably, so that he might greet the coming buddha according to the prophecy that the Maitreya Buddha will take over from Śākyamuni Buddha when the end times come. In other words, because the future will be an age of action, the coming Maitreya Buddha has been symbolically enshrined on the outside.

The past was a time of one buddha and one thousand bodhisattvas. However, because the future will be the era of a far-reaching global village, the Founding Master said that it will be a time of living buddhas, of one thousand tathāgatas and ten thousand bodhisattvas.

This "ten thousand bodhisattvas" does not literally mean ten thousand people who are bodhisattvas. Rather, it refers to the emergence of a myriad of bodhisattvas pouring forth like grains of sesame seeds. We, too, must diligently accumulate merit so that we may enter among their ranks. If we encounter this dharma but are unable to enter within it, then we are both foolish and lazy.

Anyone can become a buddha-bodhisattva if he makes a

vow and diligently accumulates merit. In the world of the past, everything valuable lay in the hands of a limited number of people. Foods such as ginseng, and items such as brass chafing dishes were the exclusive possessions of the noblest people. Today, in contrast, anyone can eat ginseng or own a brass chafing dish if that person has the mind to do so. In the same way, becoming a buddha-bodhisattva was once difficult, something that only rare and special people could accomplish. Today, we all can achieve this if we simply make up our minds and practice.

## The Life of Seeking to Possess the Il-Won-Sang

The Il-Won-Sang Vow is a sutra that instills in us the pledge to possess the Il-Won-Sang Truth.

If we do not possess this truth, if we instead set as our goals worldly values, such as money, honors, or privilege, we may find ourselves succumbing to perverse delusions or suffering terrible disaster as a result. Once we possess the truth, however, those wordly values will naturally follow even if we do not put any effort into pursuing them. For if we merely possess the Il-Won-Sang Truth, all things are contained within it.

All of us must make a vow to possess the truth and devote ourselves to achieving this. We must first seek the Way (道, *dao*), and then proceed toward ultimate bliss, earn money, and seek honors. If we do not have the Way as our foundation, we will end up being carried along by fixation and attachment. No matter what outstanding things we may do, we will end up ruining even the life to come.

I once listened to the recording of a lecture given by a shaman who was the holder of a master's degree, and who was invited to speak by the department of Eastern religions at Wonkwang University.

The speaker talked about a man who had established a prominent university in rural Korea. He was very rich and had done a great deal of welfare work—for orphanages, homes for the elderly, and so forth—as well as a lot of other social work. However, this man fell ill. He traveled all the way overseas to receive treatment at a foreign hospital, but there was no improvement in his condition and he ended up passing away.

This man had loved his youngest daughter dearly during his lifetime. Now, the late father was appearing to his daughter every night and tormenting her. "Take my soul," he said to her.

The daughter, who was a teacher, said prayers to rid herself of her father's soul, and she even received counseling from a cleric. She tried all sorts of things before finally performing a *naerimgut*—a rite to become a shaman—and, accepting her father's spirit, became a shaman herself.

At first, she had even believed her father's spirit to be a demon.

But thanks to the spirit, she could earn money and continue all of the welfare work for orphanages and the disabled that the father had done during his lifetime.

The father had done many good things for others when he was alive. Then why was his spirit not delivered?

Even though he was doing many good works, he was being carried along by fixation and attachment, rather than having a mind free of signs (false concepts) and based in truth. This became a kind of snare binding him to an evil destiny.

So we see that no matter what good deeds we may have done, we cannot be guaranteed a next life if we do not have as our foundation a mind possessed of the truth. The first thing we must do, then, is to engage in mind-practice so that we may possess the truth.

There exists something in this world that is concealed by the myriad things in heaven and earth, and the dharma realm of empty space. Confucius called it "Heaven." The ancestors of today's Koreans did not realize it, but they called it by the names of "God" and "Heaven." Buddha called it "Dharmakāya," Jesus called it "God," and the Founding Master called it "Il-Won-Sang."

The enlightened person can see the Il-Won-Sang Truth, but the unenlightened person cannot. The Founding Master is the one who awakened to this hidden truth and gave it the name of "Il-Won-Sang."

So why did he give it this name?

Il (一) means "one," that which is unique and has no other. This means that the truth is singular.

Won (圓) means that while it is one, it includes all things. This means that within it exist awesome power, all manner of blessings, and myriad creative transformations.

Sang (相) indicates that even though all things have form, the truth has none. We must awaken to the existence of this Il-Won-Sang Truth and make a firm vow to possess that truth.

We must not dismiss ourselves. Within each of us exists the seed of a buddha. Every one of us can attain buddhahood if we find that seed and cultivate it. When we fervently nurture our vow to become a buddha, it is said, the buddhas will gather in Tusita Heaven and hold an early sanctification ceremony. "With such a vow," they say, "that person is certain to become a buddha."

So how should we nurture our vow? We nurture it through supplication, we make the pledge as we attend dharma meetings, and people possessing the same believing mind and the same vow, nurture it by meeting and exchanging opinions with one another.

At the Seoul temple, there are three very large ginkgo trees. Imagine the seeds that grew into these mighty trees. They were very small. Tiny seeds grew to become those magnificent trees. Likewise, when we plant the seed of a buddha and harbor it within us, it will grow someday into the mighty tree of a buddha.

One of Master Taesan's dharma instructions is the "Verse of the Mind Prayer":

"Everywhere my hand reaches, everywhere my feet stand, everywhere my voice echoes, everywhere my heart is pointed, all of us have an affinity in attaining buddhahood and delivering sentient beings."

Every time I sing this verse, I strengthen my vow and my heart grows firmer in its pledge. Once our vow to become a buddha and deliver sentient beings has grown as solid as a rock, it is said that we can avoid all adversity from outside and pass through all torment as though crossing over a doorway. The person who has the noble and firm vow to become a buddha can overcome any evil within and attain buddhahood.

# PART I

# The Truth of Il-Won-Sang

## Outline

The Founding Master attained great enlightenment on April 28, in the first year of the Won-Buddhist Era. At that moment he said, "All things are of a single body and nature; all dharmas are of a single root source. In this regard, the Way that is free from arising nor ceasing and the principle of the retribution and response of cause and effect, being mutually grounded on each other, have formed a clear and rounded framework." This dharma instruction "The Truth of Il-Won-Sang" is where he explained the content of the Il-Won-Sang Truth in terms of its foundation and functioning.

He articulated the relationship between the truth and all things, and the way in which this relationship creates, nurtures, and transforms the myriad things in heaven and earth as it manifests changing and immutable creative transformations. The Il-Won-Sang Vow consists of two main sections, "The Truth of Il-Won-Sang" and "The Practice of Il-Won-Sang," and can therefore be examined in terms of arguments about "what is" and "what we should do." The first part, "The Truth of Il-Won-Sang," tells us how we can describe the truth.

How, ultimately, does the truth exist? Is it present in heaven?

Is it present on earth? This section speaks to the existential aspects of the philosophy that explain how exactly the truth exists and what its nature and structure are.

Looking at the vow, we can see that the Founding Master explained in great detail the nature and structure of the truth. We can therefore grasp the truth in our hands. This truth is something no one can envy us for possessing. A country has only one president, and so people fight to occupy that position. But while there is only one truth, it is a realm that both you and I can occupy. There is no need to compete for this position, nor is there any need for envy, just as we do not envy a group of people who are all looking longingly at the moon.

The truth is not limited, no matter how many people possess it. Indeed, it is all the better when it is used to the fullest extent that it is possessed.

There is a song that was popular many years ago. Its lyrics include the lines, "Who is my beloved? Where can he be? What could he be doing? I want to meet him." "The Truth of Il-Won-Sang" tells us what the truth looks like, what its nature is, and how it exists.

# Chapter One

# GENERAL CONTENT OF THE IL-WON-SANG TRUTH

> "Il-Won is the realm of samādhi beyond all words
> and speech, the gateway of birth and death
> that transcends being and nonbeing,..."

The Il-Won Truth speaks of the samādhi state when we practice Sŏn (禪, meditation or zen), something that cannot be expressed in words or language. This means that it is a realm of giving forth and taking in, transcending discriminations of "is," "is not," "good," or "bad."

This passage explains the kind of person our beloved is. In other words, it deals with the question of the content of the truth-buddha that we call Il-Won. It explains that the truth has two faces: essential nature and function. It speaks of the duality of the truth, which is singular yet at the same time has both a foundational aspect and a functional aspect. When people have two faces, they succumb to contradiction, but the Il-Won-Sang Truth possesses duality without contradiction.

Won-Buddhism takes the Il-Won-Sang Truth as its central tenet. This means that Won-Buddhism has adopted the Il-Won-Sang Truth as the source of its doctrine, and that it is a teaching that all believers regard as the object of their faith and adopt as their standard for practice. It is a very precious dharma instruction in which the Founding Master succinctly explains the content of the truth with two phrases.

## "Il-Won is the realm of samādhi beyond all words and speech ..."

The words "Il-Won is . . . beyond all words and speech" mean that it is a realm where words and language have ceased, so that one cannot teach it, one cannot imagine it in one's mind, one cannot conceptualize it, one cannot explain it through words. It is a realm of the ultimate of nonbeing, a realm of perfect bliss, a realm of utmost good, and a realm that exists before a single mind, our parents, or heaven and earth came into being.

In the *Daodejing* this realm is described with the words, "The Way that can be expressed in words is not the true Way." In other words, if we can call something the Way, it is neither an eternal Way nor an absolute Way. Ultimately, the absolute Way is one that cannot be given shape through language.

In the *Huangdi Yinfujing* we find the words, "The supremely tranquil Way cannot be matched by calendars." This means that the Way is a realm that cannot be reckoned through calculations. In Christian theology, God is of a realm unknown to us. In our own "The Dharma of Timeless Sŏn," this type of realm is called the "empty realm of true voidness."

The "realm of samādhi" refers to a genuine realm that we reach when we practice seated meditation, a realm when both subject and object become void, so that there is no "I," no "you," no "parents," no "heaven and earth." It is the state before a single mind emerges, before we emerge from our parents, before heaven and earth are divided. This means that the truth that provides the foundation for the Il-Won-Sang Truth is like a state of samādhi—an absolute oneness that we are incapable of imagining with our minds.

If we live our lives without knowledge of this realm of samādhi, we find ourselves building objects and our thoughts multiplying. For example, we might compare our children with the children of others, or if our classmate or someone close to us is promoted, we might create an object, so that our minds become turbulent, and we are troubled by many defilements and delusions.

The truth is a place of absolute oneness where objects have ceased. Thus, it is always a state of samādhi no matter how things may move—a state of samādhi through the changing of the seasons from spring to summer to fall to winter. We, too, enter a state of samādhi when our objects cease. The *Heart Sutra* describes the mental operations of "feelings, perceptions, volition, and consciousness," meaning that if we merely feel and do not perceive, we are in the samādhi without assumptions. If we merely listen and do not think, this is an early state of samādhi.

For example, if a car passes by and we hear it but do not think it noisy, that is samādhi. If we train ourselves enough with this—merely listening without thinking—we can enter samādhi wherever we happen to be. No matter how noisy and loud a sound may be, if we do not think that it is noisy and loud, it could be said that we are entering a state of samādhi without assumptions and that we have taken the first step toward becoming one with the samādhi state of truth.

If we understand the samādhi state of truth to be the type of state where there is no "you" or "I," where everything is empty, this is like understanding one half of the truth. It may be said that we must first travel to this place and back before we can travel to perfect bliss and the kingdom of God.

With God, there are no degrees of kinship. The grandson calls God "father," and the grandfather calls God "father." This is a realm without distinctions of high and low. Thus, Master Taesan gave that realm the name of "Mr. Great Equality." In the realm of truth, the buddha and all ordinary humans and sentient beings are equal.

Only when we know this realm can we understand equality and know what is true. Someone may tell us to be true to ourselves, but if we do not know this realm of samādhi, we cannot say what is true and we cannot be a true person. However, this realm is not far away, nor is it difficult to reach. If we let go of a single thought, that realm is the first step toward samādhi and the realm of essential nature.

Because there are so many people, we create objects and differentiate them in various ways. However, there is only one Il-Won-Sang Truth, and so there is nothing to objectify. If there were two Il-Won Truths in this world, the truths would differentiate each other too. Since there is but one truth, it is forever in a state of samādhi, a transcendent entity without objects. The truth is always in a state of samādhi, in past, present, and future. We therefore call this realm the truth that neither arises nor ceases.

## "…the gateway of birth and death that transcends being and nonbeing,…"

The truth is constantly working as it exists in a samādhi state. It creates and nurtures all things from an impartial position that transcends the differentiations of "existing and nonexisting," "good and bad," "right and wrong." The words "birth and death" here mean that it becomes a gateway of creative transformation that both causes all things to come into being and removes them.

Whenever we form a human relationship, we typically approach it with a fixating mind—one that views affinity as being present or absent, one that favors or despises. Thus we give and take without fairness. We give more to those we favor and do harm to those we despise, growing to hate them even more in the process. It is a common occurrence for sentient beings to fixate on hatred and love and act in a way that lacks fairness.

The Il-Won-Sang Truth, however, distributes fairly to all things from a realm that transcends notions of fondness and loathing. The words "gateway of birth and death" mean that we are punished fairly, blessed fairly, and kept alive or killed according to our actions.

I, the one delivering this lecture, have now entered the winter of life. I do not wish to grow older, yet I do find myself growing older and approaching death. If I ask, however, who it is that draws me toward old age and death in this way, I will see that it is none other than the Il-Won-Sang Truth. The truth is what pulls me toward old age and death. But the Il-Won-Sang Truth does so fairly, from a realm that transcends differentiation between favor and scorn. This is the gateway of birth and death, and its principle is that of retribution and response of cause and effect.

If the realm of samādhi is the "essential nature" that neither arises nor ceases, then the gateway of birth and death could be described as the "function" of the retribution and response of cause and effect. As a combination of these two aspects, Il-Won is said to be the realm of samādhi beyond all words and speech, as well as the gateway of birth and death that transcends being and nonbeing. In each of these, the latter part describes the former. Thus "beyond all words and speech" describes "the realm of samādhi," and "transcends being and nonbeing" describes "the gateway of birth and death."

What this says is that the Il-Won-Sang Truth, while being a state of samādhi, is not a state of samādhi in its entirety, but a gateway of birth and death that gives forth and takes in and manifests a myriad of changes. In the *Daodejing*, this type of gateway of birth and death that transcends being and nonbeing is called the "gateway of the manifold mysteries," meaning a gateway that gives forth and draws in myriad wondrous things.

I hope this important point is clear: the Il-Won-Sang Truth is one, but it consists of an "essence" realm, which is like a samādhi state that cannot be expressed in words, and a "function" realm, from which that essential nature brings about a myriad of creative transformations from a position of fairness that transcends questions of being and nonbeing, good and bad, right and wrong.

Lao-tzu's *Daodejing* includes the words, "Heaven and earth do not act from any wish to be benevolent; they deal with all things as the dogs of grass are dealt with." Here, "heaven and earth" refer to the truth, and the Il-Won-Sang Truth administers objects from a position of transcendence that does not differentiate things as being especially good or bad, useful or useless. The words "deal with all things as the dogs of grass are dealt with" do not mean that all things are treated carelessly, but that all things are administered according to their properties, without any sense of attachment or greed. When a typhoon or avalanche occurs, all of this is done at the truth's gateway of birth and death. Had the Il-Won-Sang Truth any attachment to the earth and its features, it could not do so. It kills what is to be killed and preserves what is to be preserved from a position of fairness.

A similar expression appears in the *Huangdi Yinfujing*, which says, "Heaven creates, and heaven kills. This is the principle of the Way." What this means is that heaven has a principle, and it is based on this principle that it kills and creates all things. We could say that this principle is none other than the gateway of birth and death.

There was once a famous Buddhist monk in Jangseong. When his students asked him for dharma instruction he would go up on the dharma seat, rap his dharma cane, and sit quietly for a while before finally stepping down. Every time, he would deliver his dharma instruction without speaking, and his students were feeling very frustrated. One day, they said to him, "*Seunim* (monk), give us a dharma instruction with words next time."

"Oh! Good idea," he replied cheerfully.

So he gathered the students and once again gave dharma instruction. This time, after rapping his dharma cane, he sat quietly for a long time before saying, "A caterpillar transforms into a cicada and flies away." He then stepped down off the dharma seat. Unable to grasp the meaning of his instruction, the students said, "*Seunim*, please be more specific." The monk said, "How can I speak the truth more specifically than that?"

Have you understood the two dharma instructions, the one without words and the one with words? The monk showed them the realm of samādhi that cannot be expressed in words by providing a wordless instruction, and he gave them instruction on the gateway of birth and death by telling them that "a caterpillar transforms into a cicada and flies away." Yet the students did not grasp the meaning.

When Master Naong went to China, he went to see Master Pingshan Chulin.

"Where do you come from?" Chulin asked him.

"I studied under a man named Jigong."

"What does this Jigong do?"

"He wields thousands of swords. He uses a great sword in a harmonious way."

"Let go of Jigong's sword. What does your sword look like?"

At that, Master Naong picked up his cushion and struck Chulin. As Chulin fell over, he cried out, "That damnable thief is striking me."

Master Naong then quickly helped the monk to his feet, bowed to him, and said, "I also use thousands of swords. I can give life as I will, and I can take it away."

Hearing these words, Chulin finally gave his authentication. "Your eyes are now open," he said.

In expressing the realm of samādhi, the enlightened ones of old often did things that deviated from proper etiquette, such as striking someone with a stick or pushing him over. But when expressing the realm of being, the gateway of birth and death, they observed etiquette and a fixed sequence. The place of those actions is one where the person with the eyes of the mind/truth open understands completely, but the person with eyes closed thinks of those actions as merely play-acting.

If we wish to understand the gateway of birth and death most easily, we should look to the functioning of the mind. When the mind is asleep, this is a realm of samādhi. But when we awaken and some thought arises, that mind is the gateway of birth and death.

This is a gateway of birth and death in terms of the mind, and that gateway is the principle of retribution and response of cause and effect that blesses us and leads us to transgression. Thus, we must find the Il-Won-Sang Truth within our minds rather than seeking it somewhere far outside. Outside of our minds, we may look and look until our eyes come out of our head, but if we search inside our minds we may find it very easily.

# Chapter Two

# THE IL-WON-SANG TRUTH IS THE ROOT OF ALL THINGS

"...the original source of heaven and earth, parents, fellow beings, and laws, and the nature of all buddhas, enlightened masters, ordinary humans, and sentient beings."

I mentioned before that the Il-Won-Sang Truth is one but has two faces: essential nature and function. We can also call the essential nature the realm that neither arises nor ceases, and we may also call the function the realm of retribution and response of cause and effect. The Founding Master called the single truth possessing these two aspects the "realm of the great." This realm is said to be the root of the Fourfold Grace and the original mind of all living creatures.

The single truth that controls all things in the universe is expressed with the word "original source" when speaking of objects and with the word "nature" when speaking of living creatures. Let us consider, then, where that single Il-Won-Sang Truth is located.

Christianity tells us that God exists in heaven. This is why all churches soar upward toward the sky, I guess. I wonder whether God was depicted as being in the sky because the explanation was tailored to the cognitive capabilities of the public at the time.

Where, then, does the Il-Won-Sang Truth dwell? The Founding Master said that there is no thing or place among the myriad things in heaven and earth and the dharma realm of empty space where the Il-Won-Sang Truth is not located. He said that it fills the Fourfold Grace of Heaven and Earth, Parents, Fellow Beings, and Laws. Thus the Il-Won-Sang Truth is the original source and foundation of the Fourfold Grace and the root of all buddhas, enlightened masters, ordinary humans, and sentient beings.

Once, I painted a coarse rendering of the Bodhidharma and offered it as a gift to a monk. When he said that he was paying homage to Śākyamuni Buddha in the mornings and evenings, my response—half serious, half joking—was to ask him, "If all the myriad phenomena in the universe are buddhas, why should you worship only Śākyamuni Buddha?" So on the title line above the Bodhidharma painting I wrote, "Of all the myriad phenomena in the universe, there is none that is not a buddha. What, then, am I to pay homage to?"

## "…the original source of heaven and earth, parents, fellow beings, and laws,…"

The Il-Won-Sang Truth is the fundamental principle behind all things in heaven and earth and the original source of the Fourfold Grace. Thus, the root of all things is none other than the Il-Won-Sang Truth, and the place to which all things ultimately return is the Il-Won-Sang Truth.

If we trace the waters of Seoul's Hangang River back to their source, it is said that they arise at a small spring somewhere north of Hwacheon and flow down from there. Likewise, our foundation, and the foundation of all things, lies in the Il-Won-Sang Truth, the original source of the Fourfold Grace.

If we take apart all the things in this universe, and we keep breaking them down further and further, we will find what is called the "element." And if we break that "element" down still further, we will find what is called the "atom." If we break that atom down, we find protons, neutrons, and electrons. These particles represent the world of the infinitesimal. They, too, are said to be formed out of masses of energy.

In this way, if we venture inside in search of the root of all things, we will find energy, and what governs this energy is a principle. We could say that this principle is none other than the Il-Won-Sang Truth. Thus, the foundation of all things is the Il-Won-Sang Truth.

Master Chŏngsan said that our universe is made up of three structures: spirit, energy, and substance. He presented them in that order—spirit, energy, substance—but we will look at them in the reverse order.

Substance refers to the foundational matter. This is the sort of thing we can touch and grasp with our hands. However, if we ask what it is that moves this substance, we will find that it is none other than energy. The green leaves turn yellow and red in the autumn, and this is because the cold energy of autumn is circulating. When we get upset, the energy rises up and our faces redden. It is the presence of this energy that causes matter to change and move.

How can we describe the spirit? It refers to a wise principle that moves this energy. Because of this principle, the season changes to spring and to autumn. In the spring, the warm *yang* energy goes to work creating all things, and in the autumn the cool *yin* energy forms and gathers everything back in.

The Founding Master said that this numinous principle is the Il-Won-Sang Truth. Śākyamuni Buddha said that it was the Dharmakāya Buddha; Confucius said that it was *tian*, or heaven; and Jesus called it Jehovah. The names are different, but all refer to this wise principle and signify that its foundation is singular. Only by knowing where this one truth lies can we be certain of our master.

Among the "Essential Cases for Questioning," there is one that reads, "The myriad dharmas return to one; to what does the one return?" The myriad dharmas return to the Il-Won-Sang Truth that rules over all things. But to what does that one thing return?

In Lao-tze's *Daodejing*, we find the words, "People emulate the Earth, the Earth emulates the Way, but what does the Way emulate? It emulates nature." In other words, that which returns to one thing returns once again to all things. That one thing is contained within all things.

The Dutch philosopher Spinoza is someone who spent his lifetime studying, and his life's work was spent grinding spectacle lenses. He said that God exists within all things in the universe—a perspective called "pantheism."

Zhuangzi also gave an explanation of the Way. One day, he was visited by a friend named Dongguozi who asked him, "Where is the Way?"

The reply came, "The Way is in the millet and weeds."

Hearing this, Dongguozi said, "Are you making fun of me? Tell me of the holy Way."

"The Way is also in the tiles and bricks," Zhuangzi said. This is called the "Way is everywhere" explanation.

When we attended sporting events as children, there was always a box seat section where the principal and leading members of the community would sit politely, offering their praise and issuing orders as well. We, in turn, would follow those orders. But if we imagine the truth that moves all things in the universe to be sitting in some box seat ordering us about, we have not understood the truth properly.

As a child, I believed there was something present deep within the ground that sent spring water gushing forth and supplied warmth. A few years ago, however, I read a newspaper article that described how a spaceship had studied the moon and found that there was only dust. The article said that someone who had believed that God was in Heaven was bitterly disappointed to learn this and ultimately committed suicide.

Like this, the truth lies in all things. In other words, the myriad phenomena in the universe are all the Way. Being the origin of all things, the Way does not exist in any one place, but is present within all things. Thus, the Il-Won is the Fourfold Grace, and the Fourfold Grace is all the myriad phenomena in the universe.

A student once went to visit Su-un, the founder of Cheondoism, while he was secluded in his home.

"Where does Hanullim, the Lord of Heaven, you speak of exist?" the student asked.

Su-un heard the sound of his daughter-in-law weaving hemp on a loom and said, "My daughter-in-law is the Lord of Heaven." Hence the term Innaecheon, or "humans are Heaven," in Cheondoism. But why should only human beings be the Lord of Heaven?

The Founding Master said that all things in this world are buddhas, and that when we interact with them, we should therefore present them with buddha offerings as though we were honoring the Buddha. Each of us needs to understand and awaken to the fact that the chair in which we are sitting now is a Buddha, the Il-Won-Sang Truth, and the foundation.

## "…and the nature of all buddhas, enlightened masters, ordinary humans, and sentient beings."

The Il-Won-Sang Truth is the mind-foundation and mental functioning of all living creatures. Thus, the Way is ever-abiding and unextinguished within our minds. The Founding Master told us, "Our mind-foundation is the Il-Won-Sang Truth," and that "not only people but all things are buddhas and Hanullim."

The Il-Won-Sang Truth dwells within our minds. It was there long ago, it is there now, and it will be with us in the distant future. The easiest way to find the Il-Won-Sang Truth, our master, is to look within our minds, rather than seeking it somewhere far away. The Founding Master tells us not to seek the truth outside, but to seek it within the minds.

When we commit a misdeed, we feel shame in our conscience. When we try to tell a lie, our face grows red and our heart races. Why should this be? It is because the truth-buddha within our minds is sternly judging us.

This curious buddha called "conscience" is present within every buddha, every ordinary human, every sentient being, every lowly animal. Buddha nature is not something that is less present in tiny insects and more present in buddhas. It is equally present in both. Viewed from that realm, all beings are equal.

The Chinese character for nature (性), if separated into its component parts, indicates the place where the mind (心) emerges (生).

Where do thoughts arise? Thoughts form upon our empty mind-foundation. Once formed, they linger for a while before dissipating once again.

Sometimes, a violent mind will subside, and other times a subtle mind will combine with other things to transform into a mighty will. Within the flow of time, these thoughts go away, leaving us questioning whether we ever had them at all.

This kind of mind that arises and then goes away is called the changing mind, or the discriminating mind. There is another mind that leads us to produce this discriminating mind. There is an original mind that leads us to produce all manner of thoughts. This foundation mind that causes these thoughts to emerge is called the nature that neither arises nor ceases. The Founding Master called this kind of mind the "mind-ground." The mind-ground is said to be the Il-Won-Sang mind.

The mind-ground has two natures. As mentioned before, one is the mind of essential nature that is the realm of samādhi—in other words, true voidness. The other is the mind of the gateway of birth or death, operating according to sensory conditions—in other words, marvelous existence.

In China, the Zen monk Huineng awakened to the Way and embarked on a life of wandering, avoiding the eyes of the envious. One day, he arrived at a temple. As it happened, the monks there had split into two sides and were having a debate.

Seeing a flag waving in the wind, the monks on one side said that the flag was moving, and the monks on the other said that the wind was moving. The "moving flag" monks were pointing to the phenomenon, and the "moving wind" monks were pointing to the cause behind objects.

Huineng said, "It is your minds that are moving."

An object may be present, but what meaning does it possess in life if we do not have a mind to perceive it? In the end, we are able to perceive objects because of mental functioning, so that humans experience happiness and misfortune in their lives depending on the functioning of the mind. This is to say that even in the question of whether or not an object exists, the way the object is perceived differs according to the mind's functioning. In this way, human lives ultimately have their origins in the mind.

When the Buddha said that "all things are created only by the mind," this is what he meant. So if we awaken to the way in which the mind functions, we can awaken to the Il-Won-Sang mind inherent within our minds.

Our minds are filled with all manner of notions. When we examine them closely, we see that each of these notions has its own date of birth. Every one of them has an age. The different minds that form in this way all disappear, regardless of whether they are good or bad. Thus we say that these are "minds that arise and cease." Yet the foundation mind that presides over these arising and ceasing minds is eternal. This Il-Won-Sang mind is said to harbor eternal life.

A monk once asked Master Guizong, "Who is a buddha?"

"You are a buddha," Guizong replied.

The monk opened the eyes of his mind to these words and said. "Then how do I keep my mind free from internal disturbances and external temptations? How am I to preserve my buddha?"

Guizong replied, "When there is a single speck of dust in your eye, the void-flower blooms ostentatiously." In other words, if we are to preserve our buddha, we can only see it and protect it once we have shed our fixation on and attachment to all things.

# Chapter Three

# The Changing and Immutable Creative Transformations of the Il-Won-Sang Truth

"It can form both the permanent and the impermanent: viewed as the permanent, it has unfolded into an infinite world that is ever abiding and unextinguished, just as it is and spontaneous; viewed as the impermanent, it has unfolded into an infinite world, now as progression, now as regression, here as grace arising from harm, there as harm arising from grace, by effecting transformations through the formation, subsistence, decay, and emptiness of the universe, the birth, age, sickness, and death of all things, and the six destinies in accordance with the mental and bodily functions of the four types of birth."

The passage in the Il-Won-Sang Vow that begins with "It can form both the permanent and the impermanent" and ends with "the six destinies in accordance with the mental and bodily functions of the four types of birth" could be described as explanation of how the Il-Won-Sang Truth manifests creative transformations in all things over time, and how it directs all existence.

Often, when we are practicing the truth, we grasp only that it is the original source of all things. Through this passage the Founding Master teaches us another truth, namely that the Il-Won-Sang Truth is present, manifesting endless creative transformations both changing and immutable, not only at this moment but through the eternity of time and space.

## "It can form both the permanent and the impermanent ..."

Let us examine each part of this passage and learn its principles.

To begin with, the Il-Won-Sang Truth is described as being able to "form both the permanent and the impermanent." In other words, it is that which never changes when viewed from a perspective of no change, and that which is ever-changing when viewed from a perspective where there is change.

The word "permanent" refers to the whole of truth; this

immutable realm is called the "realm of the great." The word "impermanent" indicates the changing realm of truth, called the "realm of the small."

In short, the Il-Won-Sang Truth is one, yet it has two faces. When viewed from a realm without change, it is capable of permanence, and viewed from a position with change it is capable of impermanence. In other words, it exists forever without change when viewed from the position of the realm of samādhi beyond all words and speech, and it is constantly changing, creating and nurturing all things, when viewed from the position of the gateway of birth and death that transcends being and nonbeing.

In its sum, the Il-Won-Sang Truth is permanent and yet impermanent, impermanent and yet permanent. This means that it is both the realm of samādhi and the gateway of birth and death, where the harmonious realm of the gateway of birth and death brings about the changes of creative transformation without departing from the samādhi state.

## "...viewed as the permanent..."

Let us first learn about the permanent aspect of the Il-Won-Sang Truth. This phrase could be interpreted as giving us a picture of the immutable creative transformations of the Il-Won-Sang Truth.

The Founding Master saw the Il-Won-Sang Truth as something permanent, a realm without change, and said that it has unfolded into an infinite world that is ever-abiding and unextinguished, just as it is and spontaneous. This could be taken to mean that when viewed from the perspective of the whole, the Il-Won-Sang Truth manifests creative transformation that is just as it is and unchanging through all ages in both temporal and spatial terms.

For this reason, this realm is also called the Il-Won-Sang Truth's "realm of the great." This means that the Il-Won-Sang Truth is ever-present without changing, without arising or ceasing, as it generates creative transformations in all things. Because the Il-Won-Sang Truth is not born somewhere, because it does not begin at some point, it is said to be an entity that neither arises nor ceases, that never goes away nor ends.

Imagine a balloon. The balloon is filled with air. But what happens when you press one side of the balloon with your finger? The balloon bulges outward on the other side, right? I don't know if this is what the scientists call the Law of Conservation of Mass, but this is the way of the Il-Won-Sang Truth when viewed in terms of the universe as a whole—the realm of the great.

Buddhists have a saying: "It was so in the old days, it is so now, and it will be so in the future. The past, present, and distant future are always in that place." What this says is that even if heaven and earth are turned upside down, so that heaven becomes earth and earth becomes heaven, the Il-Won-Sang Truth remains just as it is and unchanging.

Viewed from another perspective, however, all things do change. Among all things that exist in the universe, there is none that does not change within the flow of time. There is continuous change, but the whole remains as it is.

In the *Heart Sutra*, we find the words, "Neither increasing nor diminishing." The Il-Won-Sang Truth always remains just as it is; it does not increase, nor does it disappear. The truth does not appear simply because the world comes into being, and should the world come to an end the truth will not go anywhere. The truth itself is eternal and without end, regardless of what happens.

In ancient China, there was a man named Layman Pang. One day he set out for a morning walk with his daughter, Lingzhao. He saw a drop of dew on a blade of grass and recited the words of a song: "The bright shining dew upon the grass is the same as the bright shining meaning of the enlightened master."

Hearing his song, Lingzhao said sarcastically, "This yellow-toothed fellow says all kinds of crazy things."

At his daughter's jibe, Layman Pang asked, "So what would you say?"

And just as he had done, she sang, "The bright shining dew on the grass is the same as the bright shining meaning of the enlightened master."

"The bright shining dew on the grass is the same as the bright shining meaning of the enlightened master." In other words, these two things have the same origin. The Il-Won-Sang Truth is not something that is less present in the normal person or sentient being and more present in a buddha. The unchanging truth is present equally within all things.

Lately, we have seen many astonishing things with the development of genetic engineering. Before, we thought that the gene was something found only in reproductive cells. But it was proven not long ago that with modern advancements in genetic engineering technology we are now capable of extracting genes from any cell in the body. After seeing this in the news, I thought to myself, "So the Il-Won-Sang Truth has been scientifically proven."

**When a Leaf Falls in the Autumn Wind**

A monk once asked his teacher, "What is the most fundamental principle of the buddhadharma?"

The teacher answered, "The body is exposed in the iron wind."

Here, "iron wind" refers to the autumn wind, so called because it brings a metallic energy. Thus "the body is exposed in the iron wind" means that the leaves fall away in the autumn wind and only the foundation remains.

As we live our lives, we carry with us all sorts of different thoughts. Once we have aligned our minds in accordance with the principle of "the body is exposed in the iron wind,"—asking ourselves, "Am I to live my life carrying these random thoughts around?"—and let go of our perverse thoughts, all that remains is the mind-foundation, the mind-ground, revealed just as it is. When we speak of that which remains in a state before birth or death, neither arising nor ceasing, it is a symbolic expression of this realm.

The Il-Won-Sang Truth is eternal. It is harbored within all things. It exists without beginning or end, the same in the distant past, the present, and the distant future. The Founding Master described it as "eternally preserving long life over an eternity of heaven and earth." In other words, heaven and earth are eternal.

Why are heaven and earth eternal? The truth is eternal, and so they, too, are eternal based on that truth. For this reason, the Founding Master said, "It perpetually shines alone as everything passes into extinction over myriad ages." We must strive so that only that realm is revealed. This is true for all humankind and for one's own soul.

The truth possesses infinite life. When we recite the Buddha's name, we chant the words "Na-Mu A-Mi-Ta-Bul." Here, "Na-Mu" means "return," while "A-Mi-Ta-Bul" means "limitless life enlightenment," the truth that possesses eternal life.

Because the truth is harbored eternally within our own minds as well, the meaning of "Na-Mu A-Mi-Ta-Bul" is a declaration that we will return to that place. The truth is eternal, and thus I too, live my life based on that eternal truth. From this, we can understand two things: that the truth is eternal, and that our souls are also eternal.

Viewed in terms of its great body realm, the truth is concealed within all things in the past, present, and future, unfolding into an infinite world that is just as it is and spontaneous.

A student once asked a monk, "Who is a buddha?"

"You are a buddha," the monk answered.

"Then how shall I possess the buddha?"

To which the monk very simply replied, "Do not entertain perverse states of mind. Then you are preserving the buddha."

What about you? Have you found that "just-as-it-is buddha" that neither arises nor perishes?

People have grown accustomed to living within a fixed concept of time in which all things begin, exist, and end, and we accumulate life experience based on these temporal units. If we consider things a bit more deeply, however, we will see that every beginning follows some ending before it, and that every ending presages a new beginning.

In the *Huangdi Yinfujing*, there is a passage that reads, "Birth is the origin of death, and death is the origin of birth." Spring lies at the end of winter and winter lies at the end of spring, so that each of the four seasons connects with the next, endlessly cycling. We can understand eternity and unceasing nature in terms of these changes in objects, but the Il-Won-Sang Truth that causes these changes is the realm of existence that is eternally present.

## "…viewed as the impermanent …"

Up until this point, we have looked at the unchanging realm of the Il-Won-Sang Truth—that is, the permanent. Now we will learn about the impermanent, changing aspect of the Il-Won-Sang Truth.

The Il-Won-Sang Vow contains the words "viewed as the impermanent . . . it has unfolded into an infinite world." In Korean, the word meaning impermanent, "*musang,*" consists of two parts: "*mu,*" meaning without, and "*sang,*" meaning always. In other words, there is no constancy; things change.

In the past, Buddhists focused mainly on describing a realm without change—the realm of nonbeing. While it is necessary to understand the realm without change for the sake of a future world of greater awareness, we can only go about creating a richer and more vigorous life when we understand the realm of change.

## "…by effecting transformations through the formation, subsistence, decay, and emptiness of the universe …"

How does the Il-Won-Sang Truth actually change the universe?

When spring comes, leaves sprout from the ginkgo tree, all frail and tender. At some moment, though, the tree colors its leaves green, then yellow. Then, at a certain point, they fall away and disappear off to parts unknown. But one thing is clear: this leaf is not something that was absent before and suddenly came into being. It was made to sprout and grow through the absorption of water and nutrients.

All things are this way. The universe proceeds through formation, followed by subsistence of that which has formed. It lingers for a time before gradually decaying and finally disappearing into emptiness.

It is said that our Earth has now passed through its formation eon and is currently in its subsistence eon. We will be lingering here for another few billion years. After that, it will gradually begin to collapse before finally disappearing. It is not the case, however, that the Earth will simply disappear and that will be that. Rather, it will change into another form.

Cosmologists say that there was once an Ice Age on this planet. During an Ice Age, there would have been no plants or animals as there are now. Before that, however, there would have been a time when all matter existed in the form of a vast, single mass of gas. This truly would have been the universe's decay.

All things would have slowly begun to form anew amid a state of total absence, and the Earth would have started to assume its present form. This history of formation, subsistence, decay, and emptiness is created through the operation of the Il-Won-Sang Truth.

Recently, South Koreans have had the opportunity to actually see the beautiful Mt. Geumgangsan in North Korea. This mountain features many fantastic shapes of rocks and stones, with all its earth washed away and only rocks showing. Many people enjoy seeing it, but when I saw Mt. Geumgangsan, I thought to myself, "It really is old." That mountain is essentially passing through its decay eon right now. I had the sense that Mt. Geumgangsan, too, would disappear underwater before long— into nothingness.

Mt. Jirisan, in contrast, is far younger than Mt. Geumgangsan. It is rounded with earth and fleshy. Within the flow of time, Mt. Jirisan too, will ultimately become an old mountain with nothing but rock showing, just like Mt. Geumgangsan.

In this way, rivers and mountains also pass through the stages of formation, subsistence, decay, and emptiness. I am told that there is a place in Hawaii where a new mountain is being formed amid rumbling earthquakes and erupting volcanoes. This is what we call the formation eon. The Il-Won-Sang Truth manifests creative transformations through formation, subsistence, decay, and emptiness. All things and all nature transform through these four stages within the flow of time.

It takes a very long time for the universe to progress through formation, subsistence, decay, and emptiness. One might say that it is no unit of time that we can conceive of, but rather an unlimited unit of time that goes beyond our wildest imagining.

## The Principle of Change in the Universe

This world may be vast, but when we look at it closely we can see that its movements are like the clenching and unclenching of a fist. Winter could be described as the clenching, spring as a slight unclenching. Summer would be when the fingers are splayed out fully, and autumn would be a loosely clenched fist. In other words, it changes through the stages of formation, subsistence, decay, and emptiness according to the principle of alternating predominance of *yin* and *yang*.

In explaining the truth, we used the term "the reason." In other words, truth is what makes things the way they are. There exists something that makes things the way they are, and that something is "the reason." When the river flows, when the clouds scud, when steam rises, when people move, all of these are merely phenomena. The reason that these phenomena happen is none other than the Il-Won-Sang Truth.

There is a curious principle existing in this world. The things in it come in many varieties and have their own distinctive forms, yet in the end they cannot escape the curious principle that is the gateway of birth and death. The changes in this universe proceed through formation, subsistence, decay, and emptiness through the operation of direct influences: the three cycles of water, fire, and wind. It is because of these that the earth is eroded and new mountains formed.

If we look at China's Yellow River, we see grains of yellow loam mixed into its waters. This loam is said to travel along before settling on Korea's West Sea coast. As a result, the tidal flats on the West Sea are constantly growing, creating large areas of new land.

Wind that has been heated at the Earth's equatorial regions turns into a typhoon that moves implacably toward colder regions. As it moves, various things move with it. The rain falls to moisten the earth, and that rain creates changes in the Earth's surface. Oddly enough, the water is cold due to *yin* energy, while fire, being hot, is subject to the influence of *yang* energy.

As we all know, the oceans undergo rising and falling tides with the motion of the moon, due to the moon's effects on the Earth's water energy. Fire energy, too, is subject to the influences of the sun. Between these two energies of water and fire, the wind arises to influence objects and cause changes in them. Together, all of these changes are called the formation, subsistence, decay, and emptiness of the universe.

But while the three cycles of water, fire, and wind seem to change the universe through those four stages in phenomenological terms, a closer look shows us that these wheels are themselves regulated by two energies: *yin* and *yang*. These two energies are a truth corresponding to the Il-Won-Sang Truth's gateway of birth and death that transcends being and nonbeing, and the principle of retribution and response of cause and effect.

In the universe there are seasons of spring, summer, autumn, and winter, and nothing in the universe or creation escapes the influence of these seasons. Spring is when the *yang* energy comes to flourish; summer is when it is in full flight; autumn is when the *yin* energy begins to prevail; and winter is when the *yin* energy is flourishing. Thus the *yin* and *yang* energies ultimately create the four seasons through their interactions. The Founding Master called this the principle of alternating predominance of *yin* and *yang*.

The universe is vast and infinite, yet it cannot escape the truth of the creative transformations wrought by the principle of alternating predominance of *yin* and *yang*. Based on the truth of this principle, the universe is constantly changing as it unfolds into an infinite world according to the sequence of formation, subsistence, decay, and emptiness.

### "...the birth, age, sickness, and death of all things ..."

Not long ago, there was an earthquake in Iran that took the lives of many people and injured many others. Who caused this earthquake? With apologies to those who suffered from its damages, it was the Il-Won-Sang Truth that caused this earthquake through its operation.

Ordinarily, we say that a person receives divine retribution when they commit a crime. The same is true for an earthquake. Why does a person grow old? It is because of the workings of the Il-Won-Sang Truth. Birth, age, sickness, death. It is all the same.

There once was a famous Confucian scholar in the late Joseon Dynasty. One day, a gentleman told this scholar about a train that traveled between the cities of Hanyang (today's Seoul) and Jemulpo (today's Incheon). The gentlemen said that the train was pitch black, spewed huge clouds of smoke, and was tremendously strong— strong enough to carry many people.

Hearing this, the scholar's students took him to Seoul Station to see the train. The train let out a mighty roar as it pulled into the station. The scholar stared blankly before finally saying, "I thought it would be something special, but now I see that it moves through *yin* and *yang* energy."

In other words, the reason the train moved was not because it had some special characteristics, but because of the principle of alternating predominance of *yin* and *yang*. The train moved by using the force generated as *yin* pulls on *yang* and *yang* pulls on *yin*. The same is true for all things: they operate according to the principle of alternating predominance of *yin* and *yang*.

When we inhale and exhale, our respirations follow the same principle. When we feel tired at night and sleep, we do so because the *yin* energy is flourishing. And when we move about tirelessly during the day, we do so because the *yang* energy is flourishing.

Among the many nerves in our bodies are the autonomic nerves. These include nerves for sleepiness and nerves for wakefulness—the parasympathetic and sympathetic nerves, respectively. Sympathetic nerves represent *yang* energy, and so we feel awake and tense and want to move. Parasympathetic nerves represent *yin* energy, and so we want to sleep and rest. So when the sympathetic nerves are very active, the parasympathetic nerves appear and say, "It's time to rest now," and we feel sleepiness come over us. Because we have *yin* and *yang* energy, we experience action and rest as these energies change in a relationship of cause and effect.

For all of its size, the Earth is subject to centripetal and centrifugal forces. With centripetal force, energy concentrates toward the Earth's axis, while centrifugal force is an energy in which something at the center seeks to travel to the outside. The Earth is a place where these two energies, outward-directed and inward-directed, exist in an appropriate balance. The constricting energy is the *yin* energy, and the expanding energy is the *yang* energy. In short, the Earth has an appropriate harmony of *yang* and *yin* energy.

During my time as Director of the Department of General Affairs, I once bought a *moktak*, a wooden clacker. A *moktak* only produces sound when it has a groove cut into it. With some *moktak*, the groove is too narrow and they do not generate a sound. So I used a saw to cut a groove into this *moktak*. Later, I learned that the reason for this was that the wood also has a center, and it contracts toward that central portion. All principles are like this.

We need to learn to look not only at the phenomena of formation, subsistence, decay, and emptiness or birth, age, sickness, and death, but also at the principle behind them. We must awaken to the fact that the Il-Won-Sang Truth is the driving force behind these changes.

There is a truly great variety of animals, plants, and inanimate objects present on this planet. They are constantly changing, never resting for a moment.

The sequence of change is comprised of birth, age (wear and tear), sickness (breakdown), and death (disappearance). But these changes arise due to the creative transformations of the principle of retribution and response of cause and effect.

## "...and the six destinies in accordance with the mental and bodily functions of the four types of birth."

I will now discuss the changes of the four types of birth. These types of birth are categorized according to the ways in which living creatures are born: embryo-born, egg-born, dampness-born, and metamorphic.

Humans are born with an umbilical cord, and so we call them "embryo-born sentient beings." A chick is born from an egg, and so we call it an "egg-born sentient being." Because a mosquito arises from damp places, we call it a "dampness-born sentient being." And because a caterpillar becomes a chrysalis and a chrysalis becomes a moth, we call such things "metamorphic sentient beings."

These living creatures progress and regress among the six destinies according to how they have used their mind and body.

The six destinies are stages that are categorized according to the methods by which creatures live. There are three stages where there is only a soul and no body—heavenly beings, asuras, and hungry ghosts—and three where a body is also present—human beings, animals, and denizens of hell.

So why should we be born as people, or as beasts, or as ghosts? The reason is that a living creature from one of the four types of birth either progresses among the six destinies toward becoming a heavenly being or regresses toward becoming a denizen of hell in accordance with the way it uses its mind and body.

When we use our body and mind, our deeds accumulate there. In Sanskrit, this is called "karma." The entire reality of our lives—our character, our living conditions—could be described as evidence of this power of karmic action.

We do not become women because we wish to be women or men because we wish to be men. We become women or men according to karmic affinities from our previous lives. We are not tall because of a wish to be tall, but because of deeds in a previous life. Likewise, we are not ugly because of a wish to be ugly, but because of deeds in a previous life.

We created karma as a product of the mental and bodily functioning of previous lives, and the result that we see now arose out of that karma.

A person's life is not determined by his free will. This is why people so often talk of "fortune" or "destiny." When we speak of "destiny," what is happening is that my mental and bodily functions in a previous life have formed a kind of axis, and this has become my destiny.

For this reason, the way we use our mind and body is of great importance in living eternal life. But the results of this mental and bodily functioning do not appear right away; they linger in a "karma pocket" before making their appearance. Very deep within our souls is a karma storehouse, called the *ālaya-vijñāna*, where the seeds of good and evil are stored. These are called "causes."

When we speak of the retribution and response of cause and effect, this means that deeds linger as "causes," as seeds, and then, when their time comes, they manifest themselves as "effects."

If we harbor a great deal of hatred or resentment for others in our minds, many seeds of resentment and hatred for others scatter and become planted in our mind-field. Then, when we receive a body for our next life, we find seeds of resentment and hatred sprouting in spite of ourselves, and we become the kind of person who merely finds fault with others.

Where the persimmon leaf fell away in the autumn, a bud awaits that will become another persimmon leaf in the coming year.

This is what we mean when we speak of "cause." But how does this bud arise? How large or how small that bud becomes is determined by the amount of sunlight and nourishment it receives this year. The bud that absorbs a lot of nutrients will be a large leaf, and the one that absorbs few will end up limp and feeble.

Living creatures believe themselves to be in charge when they speak and use their bodies. This mental and body functioning has been called the "use of the body and mind" here, and when we use our body and mind, the results are necessarily stored up before manifesting themselves the next time around.

Now, I will explain in a bit more detail about the result: karma.

## The World of the Ālaya-vijñāna

At the very bottom of our minds is the *ālaya-vijñāna*, the storehouse of karmic seeds. Here, all of the things we have done in our present life—the products of our use of our body and mind—are stored like a tape recording. This karma is said to lie dormant, a sleeping force. When it emerges, the power to kill a person arises, or the power to love a person. This is called the "power of karmic action."

When the karmic power to kill someone is present, it is a force within the heart that compels us to kill that person at all costs, even if we risk our life doing so. This is the power of karmic action. We therefore call it a karmic obstacle, meaning that it blinds us. Because of this karma, we cannot see anything.

How, then, does karmic power form? It depends on how we have used our body and mind.

When a plane crashes, the first thing investigators do is to look for the black box. Similarly, there is a black box storing karmic power within our minds. If we locate it and open it up to see what is inside, we will find a truly vast array of things. We will be able to see whether it contains the predisposition to become a buddha one day, or the predisposition to become a thief.

We can divide this karma into two main types: unshared karma and shared karma. Unshared karma is the karma we create for ourselves, and shared karma is karma that we create with others.

Imagine the Jang family. Within this group of people, every Jang creates shared karma within the framework of "the Jangs." If some other person starts a quarrel questioning one Jang's rightness about some matter, all of the Jangs rise up together. Why should they do this? It is because they have created shared karma.

All of you sitting here at this moment are hearing the same lecture from me. You are having nearly identical thoughts and using your bodies in nearly identical ways. This is the creation of shared karma.

Many Koreans dislike the Japanese. This is because they have created shared karma. Every Korean has his own way of thinking as a Korean and creates karma based on that way of thinking. Even if we were to change bodies and be born again as an American in the next life, we would only be American in body; most likely, we would want to come to Korea, to live in Korea, and to take the Korean side on issues.

If there truly are such people, it is worth considering their previous lives. If they created shared karma as a Korean in the past and then were reborn in this life as an American or Japanese, they would long for Korea and side with Korea because they have a history from a past life.

### The Self-Caused Room and Other-Caused Room

Even as we create shared karma in this way, the results differ slightly depending on how each of us uses our body and mind. For this reason, unshared karma is bound to appear even among those who possess shared karma. Our children have created shared karma, but they assume slightly different aspects depending on their unshared karma. There is a storehouse that collects the creation of shared and unshared karma, and we can assume that there are two different rooms for storing each of these.

First, there is what we will call the "self-caused room." I sow seeds in this room when I use my mind and body. For instance, each of us has a different character. When I was younger, my classmates nicknamed me "Slowpoke." My mother would always say to me, "Would you speed up a bit when it starts to rain?"

"You were just born to move slow," she would sigh.

Perhaps the reason I move so slowly is that I did many slow things in a previous life, planting a lot of slowpoke seeds in my self-caused room. With all the easygoing seeds that I have planted in this lifetime, I am certain to be even more of a slowpoke in the next. So I am working to break that habit during this lifetime.

In this way, each of us has a different character and different gifts. Some of us have great skills, some are stylish, some have fire in their eyes, some have keen noses, and some have bright eyes. My younger brother was born to the same parents as me, but every aptitude test that he takes shows him to be oriented toward science and engineering.

I can see that my brother is very quick with calculations. As for me, I studied the humanities and am slow with numbers. Some people are good at *baduk*, and some are good at brush calligraphy. One set of parents will have children with completely different gifts.

If I deliver a lot of lectures in this life, people will call me a gifted speaker in the next. But if someone commits a lot of thefts in this life, that person will have a tendency toward thievery in the next as well. When we use our mind and body here and now, we must make a clear determination as to whether we are planting slowpoke seeds or neurotic seeds in our self-caused room, planting the seeds of buddhahood and the gift for harmony, or planting the seeds of a knack for alienating others.

A person who is impatient by nature acts the part of impatience. The impatient person feels compelled to go out and spend money even when he has none. In this way, his overall character is created because of the self-caused room. Each of us must understand that our face, our personality, our talents; all of these are the result of the emergence in this life of seeds planted in the *ālaya-vijñāna* in our previous lives.

Second, there is the other-caused room. These are the seeds sown by others. For example, if I am good to this person seated in front, a seed is planted in his other-caused room—the thought that "Rev. Jang Eung-cheol was really kind to me." If we meet again in the next life, the seed of my having been good to him in a previous life will come to the surface and sprout.

Conversely, if I do terrible things to him, another seed is planted in his other-caused room—the thought that "Rev. Jang Eung-cheol is a truly nasty person." If we meet again in the next life, that other seed will sprout up, and he will pay me back by doing harm to me. Perhaps, he will look at me askance and say, "Don't trust that guy."

The other-caused room could be described as the place where I store the things planted in my inner mind by other living creatures. So if I have done a good job of lecturing to your other-caused rooms, it is like I am storing up my happiness. I am storing blessings to receive in my next life. I hope that as you listen to my lecture, I am planting seeds in your other-caused rooms that say, "I'm really grateful to him, I really appreciate this."

So, if you meet me in your next life, I hope you will find yourself feeling me oddly appealing, wishing to buy me a cup of tea, wishing to help me.

When the seeds planted in the other-caused room reveal themselves, some of us reap the rewards of happiness and a happy environment in the next life, while there may be others who are born into an unfortunate environment and are tormented by misfortune.

The seeds planted in the self-caused room shape people's

character—their personality, their gifts, and so forth. We develop habits that shape our character. When we create for ourselves seeds that are stored within another person, we reap as we sow—receiving back in kind the good or evil we do to others. Thus we form a variety of causal affinity environments.

## Directive and Particularizing Karma

Self-created and other-created karma are formed when we use our mind and body. Accordingly, we either progress or regress among the six destinies when we enter a new life, depending on the content of our karma. Such is the importance of our mental and bodily functioning.

When we create karma, we create many different kinds at once. We create it both thoughtfully and thoughtlessly.

Among these, there is one kind of karma that carries us around. We call this "directive karma." We are born male or female, human or animal, in accordance with this directive karma. After we have become a person, another kind of karma, an embellishing karma, leads us to become a pretty person or an ugly one, a person with large eyes or small eyes. This is particularizing karma.

The president is the leader who guides this country. Depending on how he does so, the country's conditions may improve, or they may decline. You could say that the aforementioned directive karma is like the president guiding us, and that the particularizing karma I referred to after that is like the citizens of the country.

There is something within our minds that serves as the principal force carrying us along. It may be greed, or it may be aspiration. When we are young, we follow the opposite sex around, and when we are of age we are led by our work.

What carries us around in this way is directive karma. How is a person reborn after he dies? We receive a body according to our attachments. Those attachments are our directive karma. Accordingly, we may be born into the Lee family or the Park family, we may receive a human body, or we may become a ghost.

When we look into our minds, we will find a variety of different minds there, but the strongest of these is the "commander mind." It was this mind that brought all of you here today.

We must therefore endeavor to understand what consciousness it is that carries each of us around every day. If I draw myself in a worthy direction, I will use my mind and body in worthy ways. Conversely, if I draw myself in an unworthy direction, an inferior character and poor environment will ultimately take shape.

We see women around us who are like men, and men who are like women. It is all very confusing. The reason for this has to do with directive and particularizing karma. Suppose that someone creates timid and delicate particularizing karma in life as a woman does, but that this person detests timidity and longs to possess the coarse personality of a man. If the critical consciousness of becoming that way is strong, the result of this directive karma is that one will become a feminine man.

We see families where most of the members have a gentle character, yet there is a child among them who has a very different personality. In this case as well, we see someone who has habitually engaged in coarse-natured activities over a long period of time. At some point, that person wishes for gentleness and kindness, and establishes a firm resolve to become that way. This determination, in turn, becomes a major factor in the yearning to become part of a kind and gentle family, when changing lives. So that person is born into such a family. We call the thing that causes us to be born this way our "attachment," or directive karma. When this happens, we are born into a place with a character that does not suit our own, and the old coarse behaviors gradually begin to manifest themselves once again. This is what we mean by "particularizing karma."

## "... now as progression, now as regression ..."

What is the path of progression as we live our present life? We encounter the ordinary grade, the grade of special faith, the grade of the battle between dharma and Māra, the status of dharma strong and Māra defeated, the status of beyond the household, and the status of the greatly enlightened tathāgata, when we have attended properly to our mental and bodily functioning. We progress or regress after death because of the workings of the cycle of the six destinies.

The greatest progression is to receive a human body. It is nice to be born a heavenly being, but when this happens it is no longer easy for us to create blessings.

When we are unable to create blessings, we become susceptible to corruption. Just as we have to pay more money for a hotel room with good facilities, a day in heaven is like several centuries here. Heaven, then, is a place for spending blessings, not creating them.

Revered teachers such as the Founding Master, Master Chŏngsan, and Master Taesan emerged in Korea as though stepping through a threshold to open the door for a new age and a new religion. In order to create a better world, they made promises to one another and formed causal affinities.

Thus our causal affinities are not personal ones, but ones created with the Founding Master. Likewise, buddhas undertook great efforts to create the order of *Won*-Buddhism. Now that we have found *Won*-Buddhism, we must work hard at mind-practice toward the proper use of body and mind so that we can progress.

Whether we progress or regress depends on the functioning of our body and mind. Among the people we encounter, we find those who are in a progression period and those who are in a regression period. Likewise, when we visit someone's house, we find houses where the energy somehow seems dissipated and others where the energy seems to be progressively concentrating. In other words, some houses are in a progression period, and others are in a regression period.

The person in a progression period has a thorough belief and vow to attain buddhahood and deliver sentient beings. This person is humble and deeply committed to contributing to the public good and performing acts of charity. If such a person dies and is fated to go to a bad place, the heavenly beings and asuras will intervene to guide the soul toward a good place. "Is it right for a person like you who has done such good deeds to go to such a place?" they will say. In contrast, the person in a regression phase, one who has harmed others and done many bad things, will be guided toward a bad place, even if this requires the use of temptation by the heavenly beings and asuras.

So each of us has to clearly determine whether we are, in fact, in a progression period or in a regression period, and to make a vow and change course toward a progression period.

When we are heading downhill, we have regression period thoughts when using mind and body. What the *kyomu* (Won-Buddhist clergy) says feels like the same thing we heard a few days ago, and we feel bored and frustrated, which leaves us feeling annoyed and resentful.

If we keep finding ourselves making excuses about doing

worthy things, we need to awaken to the fact that we are heading downhill. We must gather ourselves together and pray with a good mind, changing the functioning of our body and mind.

I once knew someone who was truly unlovable. This person was always being excluded for doing unlovable things. A teacher saw this and said, "I am going to write a prayer for other people. I want you to offer up this prayer and practice doing things for others, even if they are only very small things." This person accepted the teacher's counsel and prayed for three months, doing only good things for other people. At some point, people began looking at this person differently. "This is a truly lovable person," they said.

Even someone who has no loveliness within can develop it by praying to move into a progression period and using body and mind for the sake of others. Each of us needs to wipe the past clean and think deeply about whether we are doing things for others right now or harming them.

If someone says to us that we have no charitable spirit, we should think to ourselves, "Oh no, I must be in a regression period." And we should pray for all living creatures and work hard to help other people, even in the smallest ways. If we allow bad habits to influence the way we use our mind, we should say, "I must be in a regression period," and then we must change our mind and develop good habits, boldly setting our course for a progression period.

There is a story that I heard a long time back. Once, there was a famous dictionary in ancient China which was made by Emperor Longxi and called the "Longxi Dictionary of Chinese." Now, this emperor had no eyebrows, like a leper, and it turned out that in a past life he had been a leper who lived near Luoyang.

In this past life when he was a leper, the emperor had nowhere to go to find food. "I should just die," he thought to himself. He met a monk and told the monk of this, and the monk said to him, "Instead of feeling like you want to die, you would do better to perform charitable acts for others and say prayers for the country's prosperity and the welfare of its people."

Every time they met, the monk said the same thing. Finally, the leper thought, "Praying is better than dying, even if I have to beg for food." So he prayed and prayed for the country and its people, all the way from the age of sixteen to the age of eighty. Every time he begged for food, he prayed for the person from whom he was begging. Although he was a leper, he prayed and lived the life of practice for so long that he earned the name of *laishen*—"the leper god." It is said that after he died he was born into a royal family, in his next life, where he would become Emperor Longxi.

Our karmic retribution may be humble now, but we can free ourselves from the cycle of the six destinies through the way we use our body and mind. It depends on whether we are using our body and mind for ourselves now, using them for others, or using them for the country.

When we use body and mind for others or for the country, we may be using them on our own, but that energy is transmitted through a wireless telephone service: the truth.

## The Principle of the World's Creation and Destruction, Prosperity and Decay

Previously, I explained about unshared karma, which we create ourselves, and shared karma, which many people create together. Shared karma describes the karma hidden within each member of a family when that family lives together and uses body and mind as one in response to sensory conditions.

When we look closely at families, we will see the distinctive consciousness flowing within each member. It may also have its own particular value system. There exists what we call a "community consciousness." This is the manifestation here and now of the ways in which the members used body and mind as one while living together in a past life.

Some families are in a process of progressive collapse. We find households that are disintegrating, and others that are prospering in some way, with blessings and good fortune opening up for them. In these cases as well, we must turn our attention to karma from a previous life.

The head of the family works hard in every way for the sake of his family, but things do not simply go according to his wishes. When this happens, it is because there was some point in the past at which all the members of the family created shared karma in a previous life, and it is now coming back to them.

On the other hand, when the head of the family has outstanding capabilities and dharma power, he can have that great misfortune reduced to a smaller misfortune. If all of the believers sitting here today pray and pray for their family, work diligently, and demonstrate leadership ability—for example, by uniting the minds of their family members—they can achieve advancement in leaps and bounds based on karmic power from a previous life.

What is important here is that the reliability and leadership ability of the family's head will be crucial factors in this.

We also see a great many organizations in this world. There are religious organizations and social organizations, and their process of creation and destruction, prosperity and decay, is likewise determined by the results of shared karma, with the spirit of the organization leader being a factor of major importance.

The same is true for a country. In the past, the Korean people did not perpetrate atrocities such as invading other countries, but they certainly have experienced much depredation at the hands of their neighbors. How long were we forced to endure this misfortune throughout our history? Yet even in that case, it is likely the case that the effects of jointly created karmic power ultimately account for around 70 to 80 percent of it.

Regardless of the past, we continue creating shared karma even now. We are forming a new "ethnic consciousness," building the unique cultural consciousness of the "white-clad folk." Our allies—the United States, Russia, China, Japan, and so forth— bring all manner of sensory conditions upon this country. Thus Koreans use mind and body together, whether in despising or in welcoming. Sometimes, the results of this appear immediately, and sometimes the hidden consciousness is planted jointly, lingering as shared karma before the corresponding outcome arrives at some point in the distant future.

Some scholars say that all people form their own cultural consciousness. This is true, but while the shared karmic power of a people is indeed influenced by individuals, even greater influences are the leadership and response capabilities of its leaders. Recently, mass communication, too, has become an element with an increasingly large impact.

So the leaders at the helm of society must be attentive to shared karmic power. If a leader dwells too much on immediate results and creates the wrong sort of karma today, this could bring about a catastrophe in the distant future. A great leader can only create an eternally happy organization or country when he governs it with leadership grounded in morality and a sagelike use of the mind.

## "... here as grace arising from harm, there as harm arising from grace ..."

The words "grace arising from harm" mean that it is possible for grace to emerge even amid harmful conditions if we use body and mind well. Imagine someone who was born into a very poor and deprived environment. This person makes up his mind and says, "I need to sleep less than other people and work harder because I'm poor." He then goes on to succeed on the basis of hard work. This is an example of creating grace out of harm.

We may be ugly, but if we resolve to make up for it through kindness, we can create greater grace for ourselves even with an unsightly face, but if we use ugliness as an excuse to live an ugly life, we will go from suffering to worse suffering. All of this depends upon how awakened we are in our use of body and mind.

To be precise, what we call "harm" is actually bad karma that we created in a past life through improper use of body and mind, manifesting itself as reality when the time comes.

For example, it is always a problem to have an undesirable personality. It is a problem to have a humble appearance. It is a problem to be born into the midst of conflicted human relationships. An economically deprived environment is harmful and painful to people. Of course, it may be the case that just part of this is harmful, or that everything is painful.

I may live amid a painful environment, but if I believe and awaken to the fact that this harmful environment is all the result of what I have made for myself, if I content myself and awaken myself and set the proper direction for my future, committing myself sincerely with a firm determination, I can use that harm as a kind of fertilizer and transform my situation into a pleasurable one.

"I never would have recognized you." We find ourselves saying these words sometimes when we know someone to be a bit of a rascal, only to meet him again a few years later and find that he has fixed his mind, so that we hold him in much higher esteem.

What is important here, I believe, is firm will and determination, and the commitment to carry on until our wish is fully realized.

Looking back over the history of Korea, we can see that it has been a history of tremendous hardship: a small patch of land, a divided homeland, a lack of resources, and in the aftermath of the Korean War, not what you would call a good international environment. In spite of this, the ruling and working classes have banded together to overcome these difficulties and we are now poised to enter the ranks of the advanced nations.

Just from this one example of Korean history, we can see that grace is capable of forming in a harmful environment.

Conversely, "harm arising from grace" means that it is possible for damaging things to arise out of grace. In other words, if we are neglectful while existing in a place of grace, we may find ourselves facing a far more difficult failure.

If someone who has everything—a good home environment, good looks, economic means—fails to understand the value of money and time and develops the habit of not working hard and of being profligate, these bad habits will often destroy him and his family.

When we experience favorable conditions they mean that the good karma that we stored up in a previous life through hard work has come back to us in the form of a good environment here and now.

If, however, we have not awakened to cause and effect, all of the good habits we strived to form in our past life gradually turn into harmful ones—habits such as laziness and wastefulness.

Often, ordinary humans and sentient beings who have experienced a small measure of success forget all about their previous difficulties. They bask in their success, only to succumb once again to torment. As that torment deepens, they repeat the process of making a determination and striving. As though riding a seesaw, they live their lives moving up and down on the plank of creation and destruction, prosperity and decay.

However, the person who has awakened to the truth of eternal life and the truth of cause and effect knows how to progress towards self-development, and to use mind and body in a way that brings grace, without having to rise and fall on the plank of good and ill fortune. Likewise, when we study the Il-Won-Sang Truth, it is in the hope of using body and mind properly, so that we may forever progress and enjoy the grace of everyone.

### "…it has unfolded into an infinite world…"

This phrase tells us that when viewed as the permanent, whether from a perspective that takes the world as an unchanging whole or from the perspective of a truth ruling over this world, it is eternal and unfolds into an infinite world. I explained this matter earlier. Here, it is saying that an eternal world unfolds even when this world is examined from a perspective of change.

This can be described as the polar opposite of the world-view that states the world has a beginning and an end, postulating that it started when God created the world, and that it will disappear at some time in the future.

From the perspective of the *Won*-Buddhism doctrine, this changing world unfolds into an infinite world, where end and beginning link together in an endless cycle. The universe transforms as heaven and earth cause changes in one another. It unfolds into an infinite world through a process of formation, subsistence, decay, and emptiness, of spring, summer, autumn, and winter, with every beginning linked to every ending in an endless cycle.

It must be understood, however, that I am not talking about the turning of some kind of hamster wheel. It is an eternal continuation. It is like when winter ends and spring arrives, but while this year's spring is the same as last year's, in terms of its being spring, it differs slightly in its content.

The same is true of the stages of formation, subsistence, decay, and emptiness. All things, being senseless, change through a process of birth, age, sickness, and death within the greater framework of heaven and earth.

When I was a child, my family ran a mill, where one large wheel would be turning vigorously, and a great number of smaller wheels turning with it. In the same way, all things are constantly changing based on the larger framework of heaven and earth.

Next, there is the world of living creatures. While the soul itself is eternal, existing infinitely without beginning or end, its content, its position, and so forth—these things are forever changing. These changes center on mental and bodily functioning grounded in the changes of the universe, so that the change proceeds eternally—sometimes as progression, sometimes as regression.

What we must note here, however, is that even though the universe and all things change mechanically according to a certain timetable, living creatures may live longer or shorter lives depending on how they use their minds, based on the mechanical changes of the universe. This is why mind-practice is such an important factor in our lives.

When we make proper use of mind and body, we can create good karma and live for many years, developing an even more outstanding character and earning respect. If, however, we do not manage our minds properly, we will create the wrong karma and become corrupt or regress.

How are all of us here using our minds for ourselves? How are we using them for our family, our temple, our world? We write our own histories. At this moment, each of us is writing our history.

The past is gone, and the future has yet to arrive. It is only ever this moment. There is no past, no future; only this moment. We create our history by the way we use our minds at this moment.

In what direction are we steering our life, toward desire, toward pursuit of the truth? We must set the proper course here and now. We must think and act with a whole mind. Using our minds for others is the path to benefiting ourselves. Only when we use mind and body to change our bad habits to good ones can we change course toward progression.

How much fresher is the dharma instruction of Master Chŏngsan, who said, "Engage in proper mind-practice so that you become a master in the new world."

# PART II

# The Practice of Il-Won-Sang

## Outline

The Founding Master experienced the great enlightenment of the truth and gave it the name of Il-Won-Sang. In the section on truth, he explained the realms of the Il-Won-Sang Truth—the realm of samādhi and the gateway of birth and death. He said that this is the foundational principle of all things in the universe and the nature of all living creatures, and that it manifests changing and immutable creative transformations over time through all things in the universe.

In this section on the practice of Il-Won-Sang, the Founding Master could be said to explain to later generations how they should embody the Il-Won-Sang Truth in their lives. The gist of this section is a dharma instruction exhorting us to accept the Il-Won-Sang as our object of faith and adopt it as a model for our practice, guarding our minds, understanding human affairs and universal principles, and using our minds properly so that we instill a consummate character, gain the awesome power of

# THE PRACTICE OF IL-WON-SANG

Il-Won, and commit ourselves to unifying with its substance and nature.

Owing to a lack of knowledge in the past, the main stream of religious activities in those days consisted of teaching people merely to believe in the truth of the universe or the scriptures of sages. This could be characterized as "faith and work religion." Because the world of the future will be one of clearer awareness, there will be a major emergence of "practice religion"— religion that goes beyond mere faith and extends to belief in and awakening to the truth of the universe, as well as practice of this in our daily lives.

As such, the section on practice could also be described as offering an explicit methodology for attaining buddhahood: a life of using the truth immanent within the universe as something of one's own.

# Chapter Four

# A LIFE MODELED WHOLEHEARTEDLY ON THE IL-WON-SANG TRUTH

"...modeling ourselves wholeheartedly on
this Il-Won-Sang, the Dharmakāya Buddha,
...we deluded beings..."

Those deluded beings who have not awakened to the truth must adopt the Dharmakāya Buddha Il-Won-Sang Truth as their object of faith and model for practice, as explained by the Founding Master, and cultivate their lives into those of buddhas and sages.

First, we must consider where we place our trust as we live our lives. When troubles arise, we often find ourselves crying out to our parents. This is because we depended upon them from the earliest stages of childhood, and they assumed a place in our unconscious as a refuge to turn to in times of trouble.

While we may place this trust in our parents, at some point we must leave their nest. In my own experience, the despair that I felt when I sensed my mother's helplessness was truly devastating. When our faith in our parents goes away, it gradually shifts over to our spouse.

Some time ago, the wife of one of my *Won*-Buddhist acquaintances passed into nirvana. He told me that he could not bear to enter the room where she had lain on her sickbed. He was unable to enter, he said, because of a feeling of emptiness. It was as though some kind of wall against which he had been leaning had collapsed, but the refuge that a wife or husband represents is destined to collapse in the end.

Some people place their faith in their children, but are our children worthy of our faith? In the end, they too, will marry and leave us, offering us only the sorrow of parting. Still less, can we put our trust in money or possessions, or in glory and power? All of them will collapse, vanish, and scatter to the wind at some point.

When we come to depend upon something that we cannot possibly expect to stay with us forever, we are no different from a small child playing house against a collapsing wall.

It may be said that when we live our lives believing in and

depending upon those things that we can touch and see, this eventually becomes the seed of misfortune. I recall the lyrics of a popular song many years ago: "Love is the seed of tears." When we love money, love glory, love the opposite sex, we may feel pleasure from attaining those things, but before long we are forced to endure the pain of separation because of that love. We must avoid such deluded behavior.

Even greater misfortune befalls those who place their faith in superstition, such as shamans, or their own vain selves. Thus far in human history, we have lived through our infancy and adolescence. Because of this, many high-order religions have been unable to accurately teach people the faith of truth. They have gone no farther than the worship of individual sages, failing to present the real truth and engaging in personification, which has given rise, in turn, to distortion of the truth faith and all of the errors that come with that. A large part of the blame for this appears to lie with the delusions of the public.

So what are we to believe? In his chapter on "The Founding Motive of the Teaching," the Founding Master instructed us to believe in a religion based in truth. It may be rational to believe in the teachings of a sage who has achieved awakening, but it is a contradiction to take that sage as an object of faith and pray to him for blessings and happiness.

For if we pray to a sage, the sage's power to actually grant blessings and happiness is limited. It may be said that we only become the most ideal practitioners and perform acts of faith most in line with principles when our object of faith is the realm of Il-Won-Sang Truth, which rules over and transforms all things in the universe.

The Founding Master taught us that even if someone can erect memorial statues to commemorate his contributions, he should not be the object of worship—that the only object of worship can be the Il-Won-Sang Truth that governs all things in the universe.

This may be the most revolutionary statement in the history of human religion. Now, Il-Won-Sang faith is somewhat difficult. All of you here surely experienced this in the beginning.

We are predisposed to dedicate our faith to the buddha image that we can see with our eyes. The Dharmakāya Buddha Fourfold Grace seems unclear at first because we cannot see it with our eyes or hear it with our ears. But while we may enshrine the Il-Won-Sang through images at first, over time we should recite the words "Dharmakāya Buddha Fourfold Grace" repeatedly, and when we experience difficult things, trying things, pleasant things, difficulty making decisions, we should pray and pray while thinking about the divinity and mercy of the Dharmakāya Buddha Fourfold Grace. If we do so, we will eventually come to perceive the Il-Won-Sang Truth with our mind. It is a process of coming to serve the Il-Won-Sang Truth with our mind. When we reach this point, we can feel how the truth-buddha is always there, protecting us and chiding us when we set upon the wrong path.

Moreover, when we are committed in our life of faith and devote ourselves to mental affirmation and formal prayer, we develop a sense of connection with the formless Dharmakāya Buddha Fourfold Grace through our mind. Truly amazing advances have been realized recently in wireless telephone technology with the cell phone. If it were possible for someone to have a wireless telephone conversation with the Dharmakāya Buddha, as though they were speaking to one another without a telephone line, we might say that he has gained the awesome power of the truth-buddha.

When a prayer comes from someone who senses the power of the Dharmakāya Buddha Fourfold Grace, it is responded to more quickly, and that which the person desires comes to pass.

## Belief in the Truth, Doctrine, Order, and Teacher

If we are to arrive at the aforementioned faith in the truth and perception of its awesome power, our beliefs must work in tandem. These are the Four Great Beliefs of Nonduality: belief in the truth, the teacher, the doctrine, and the order.

When we practice our faith fervently with this fourfold belief, our path to faith in the Il-Won-Sang Truth, the ultimate stage, will be swift. I will therefore introduce it to all believers and ask that you believe in it together.

If you go to the airport, you will see that an airplane does not immediately soar up into the ether. Rather, it races along the runway before finally making its leap up into the sky. Similarly, there must be an accompanying stage of belief if we are to arrive at perfect faith.

First, there is the path of belief in teachers. The Il-Won-Sang Truth is a very mysterious absolute: it is invisible to the eye, makes no sound, gives off no smell, and cannot be touched. It is important for us to have a mind of faith oriented toward believing in the dharma power of those teachers and obeying their teachings: the Prime Dharma Masters who guided us by their believing in, being awakened to, and practicing the dharma of the Founding Master; the teacher who experienced the great enlightenment of the Il-Won-Sang Truth and taught us to enable ourselves to practice it; and teachers of superior dharma rank.

Second, we must have profound faith in the order created by these teachers. Without the order, it would be impossible to offer effective succor to the world, and none of us could receive deliverance forever. The order will be a beacon for humanity and a training ground for attaining buddhahood, developing many sentient beings into buddha-bodhisattvas. We must therefore participate in the order with a faith that is united and devoid of differentiation, forming an ever closer affinity with the buddha and striving for the order to become a field of blessings, united in reverence of the Buddha's works.

Third, we must put our faith in the doctrine, system, and teachings left behind by the Founding Master. We must be profound and sincere in our belief. Each of us should become one with the doctrine, developing such appreciation that our mind-set is not one of "sort of liking," but one of rejoicing and exultation. For the most part, our minds have become tainted by worldly values.

I recall the story of one follower of *Won*-Buddhism. Before this person encountered the faith, a lucky day meant being able to get a free cup of tea from somebody. But after encountering *Won*-Buddhism and commencing study of the truth of retribution and response of cause and effect, this person came to believe that the luckiest day was one of being able to perform some charitable service for others.

In this way, our values must change so that they conform to the doctrine of *Won*-Buddhism. Only when our philosophy of life changes in accordance with the teaching of *Won*-Buddhism will we be born as a new buddha-bodhisattva and enjoy the respect of others.

Fourth, we must have a belief that is one with the truth. With each passing day and each passing month, we must develop a mind of faith that reveres, relies upon, and unifies with the Dharmakāya Buddha Fourfold Grace, the ultimate being that exists in nature, which shelters and nurtures us through today, tomorrow, and yesterday and sternly punishes us when we err. Before, I made mention of the mind of faith in the truth.

When we live without belief in the Won-Buddhist doctrine, teachers, order, and truth, it is as though we are sailing without knowing to which port we should travel. It is as though we are walking in the darkness of night without a lamp. But when we proceed with faith, our life will become one of following a beacon and knowing all the signposts.

There are not parents in this world who would abandon the children who believe in and depend on them. When a sentient being has sincere faith in a teacher, that teacher will never desert the student. Instead that teacher will look after and instruct the student. Likewise, the sentient being, who has faith in the order, will never be abandoned by it, and the buddha-bodhisattva who gave us the doctrine will deliver, without exception, those believers who have sincere faith in it.

When we have endless faith in the Dharmakāya Buddha Fourfold Grace, we enjoy the hidden help and virtue of the truth. We must impress this fact deeply upon our mind. Faith should not be tallied in terms of immediate interests and profits. Limitless blessings and virtue only come when we have dedicated a belief that transcends issues of interests and profits.

## Awakening to the Delusions of Sentient Beings

We must begin by recognizing that we are deluded sentient beings.

Delusion means, first, not knowing that one is buddha; second, not understanding the principle of the cycle of the six destinies and the principle that lives eternally; third, being unaware of the existence of the ever-bright and ever-numinuous principle of retribution and response of cause and effect; and fourth, not knowing how to escape from this delusion. Thus delusion is a lack of knowledge about the dharma of practice and the dharma of creating blessings. It is only when we recognize this delusion that faith emerges and we can practice with humble minds.

The *Diamond Sutra* tells us that the person who has observed the precepts and cultivated merits, joining the order of one buddha, two buddhas, countless buddhas, will love and praise the buddha-dharma even when the end of the Earth comes.

On a different note, before the emergence of *Won*-Buddhism there were many sages who emerged in Korea to perform its role.

The first of these was Choe Su-un, who came to the world in Yongdam, Gyeongju, and laid the groundwork. Su-un has been called the "Yongdam god of gratitude," and his role was to show a new possibility for religion, aspiring to achieve new changes in a traditional Korean society where the old customs of the past lay fallow like an abandoned field.

Next, there is Gang Jeung-san, called the "Donggok god of exorcising resentment." Gang's role was as a major sage in the Donggok area of Jeonju. His activity consisted mainly of resolving grievances and the injustices that had been perpetrated over the years.

Following Su-un and Jeung-san, came the Founding Master, called the "Yeongsan and Iksan god of the myriad sages," a presiding sage who would make sages of us deluded sentient beings.

When Śākyamuni Buddha arrived in this world, there had already been many others, including Master Jing-wi, who had come before to lay the foundation. In Christianity, John the Baptist came into the world and did his work ahead of Jesus Christ.

As these examples show, before the arrival of a great order there are those who come to lay the groundwork, after which presiding buddhas arrive to carry out their work. The Founding Master came to initiate a new order and make sages of sentient beings.

The doctrine of *Won*-Buddhism consists of a method of practice for making all of us into sages. It is important, then, that we understand this fundamental meaning and embark on our practice after first making a vow to escape the delusion of the sentient being and become a sage.

There was a time when I served for a while directly under Master Taesan. He slept in the main room, and I slept in an attached side room. How would I, a deluded sentient being, have felt serving and sleeping next to Jesus Christ? I will never forget the moment when I considered what an honor it would have been to serve and sleep next to Śākyamuni Buddha. I felt overcome with emotion. "Oh!" I thought, "To be able to serve and sleep next to Master Taesan. . . ."

In the past, it was not possible to meet sages. In the future, however, it will be a world in which we shake hands with sages, eat with them, and interact with them directly. For this to happen, we will need to open our eyes. We will only meet sages if we become sages ourselves. Here and now, there is no question of our being wanting, of our being humble, or coming from a poor family. All that matters is that we firmly resolve to achieve buddhahood through mind-practice based on this method.

## The Relationship between the Dharmakāya Buddha and the Il-Won-Sang

Why did the Founding Master talk about "deluded beings modeling themselves wholeheartedly on this Il-Won-Sang, the Dharmakāya Buddha"? Isn't it a bit odd that he would suddenly start talking about the "Dharmakāya Buddha"?

All of the sages of the three periods of past, present, and future have roots. A sage without roots is a second-rate sage. For instance, Jesus traced his roots back to the figure of Moses in Judaism. The Old Testament was a collection of Judaic scriptures assembled by the disciples of Jesus Christ in his spirit.

However, didn't Judaism persecute Christianity terribly? Even so, there were very discerning people among the disciples of Jesus Christ, and Christianity avoided abandoning its roots in Judaism by adopting its scriptures as the Old Testament.

What were the Buddha's roots, or who did he take as his guide? It was Dīpaṃkara Buddha. He is a figure we know today from Hinduism. Buddhism absorbed a great deal from the Hindu scriptures. Confucius also made it clear that his roots lay in the ideas of Yao, Shun, Yu, Tang, King Wen, King Wu, and the Duke of Zhou.

In other words, a sage without roots can never be a first-rate sage, and his religion will merely be transitory. We can distinguish between temporary religions and eternal ones based on whether or not they have roots. A temporary religion is like a blade of grass that shoots up quickly in the summer but withers away in the fall.

The Founding Master predicted that the world of the future would have a dominant religion whose principal figure would be the buddhadharma. However, he also said that it would have to be not the old Buddhism, the one fragmented into different sects, but a new

Buddhism adapted to everyday life, the public, and the times.

The great scholars are not those who claim originality, but those who show humility and serve their predecessors, those who have studied under a teacher and realized new achievements based on that teacher's ideas.

A noted calligrapher will always tell you the teacher under whom he studied. Religion is no exception to this rule. It seems that the dharma of using mind of the sage is such that even when that sage achieves an original enlightenment, he must show respect for those who came before and carry on the line between past, present, and future.

The Founding Master was also able to claim originality, presenting a system centering on the doctrine of the Fourfold Grace, the Four Essentials, the Threefold Study, and the Eight Articles, with the Il-Won-Sang as a fundamental tenet. The fact that he traced his roots to a predecessor in the form of Śākyamuni Buddha seems to reflect a spirit of great cause penetrating equally among all sages of the triple world of past, present, and future, and a sense of loyalty between one sage and another.

There are two sayings frequently used among Buddhists: "The brilliance of the Buddha increases each day (佛日增輝)," and "The dharma wheel turns again (法輪復傳)."

"The brilliance of the Buddha increases each day" is spoken between students of Śākyamuni Buddha. It means that great teachers like Bodhidharma, Huineng, and Venerable Wonhyo carried on the buddha light of Śākyamuni Buddha and worked ceaselessly to make it shine ever brighter.

"The dharma wheel turns again" means "to shed new light upon and keep turning the dharma wheel as Śākyamuni Buddha did for Dīpaṃkara Buddha before him." Before Jesus Christ, there was Moses. We might say that Jesus traced his roots to a previous sage in the form of Moses.

Thus "The brilliance of the Buddha increases each day" indicates transmission in smaller units, and "The dharma wheel turns again" indicates a give-and-take between presiding sages within a grander scheme, one in which one great era changes completely.

When the Founding Master traced his roots back to Śākyamuni Buddha, this was an example of "The dharma wheel turns again" rather than "The brilliance of the Buddha increases each day." We must understand that he did not trace his roots to any Korean master; he went back thousands of years to the source of Śākyamuni Buddha.

It is therefore necessary to understand that the Founding Master used both phrases of the Il-Won-Sang Truth to which he himself awakened and the Dharmakāya Buddha realized and elucidated by Śākyamuni Buddha, thus making clear the original guiding Buddha.

# Modeling Oneself Wholeheartedly on the Dharmakāya Buddha Il-Won-Sang

Modeling oneself wholeheartedly means adopting an object of faith and a standard for practice. Ordinary people live according to their desires, whatever those may be. A somewhat more advanced person learns from books and family tradition, adopting those as standards for living.

An even wiser person turns to religion and adopts religious teachings as a standard. Who do all of you look to in your lives? You must think about whether you are looking to people or objects, or whether you are looking to the truth.

What does a buddha regard as a standard in life? A buddha adopts the truth as a standard. Thus it was the truth that created the buddha. We can only hope to imitate it if we consciously work to emulate it with our practice.

Of course, even those who merely come into contact with Won-Buddhism regularly will unwittingly come to imitate it a great deal. But doing so takes too much time. We need to consciously make up our minds and strive to emulate it. This is the only effective means of doing so. This effort is of paramount importance.

Modeling oneself wholeheartedly on the Dharmakāya Buddha Il-Won-Sang does not mean coming to resemble it without any effort on our part. It means setting standards for ourselves and working to emulate it.

If we go to a temple, we can see the Buddha carrying other buddhas on his head. In other words, the Buddha lives with other buddhas on his head so that he might come to emulate the use of mind by buddhas who have achieved enlightenment.

When we carry our teachers on our head, hold them to our breast, and make active efforts to emulate them, we will discover the mind-truth unseen as truth, adopt it as our standard, and come to resemble it.

# Chapter Five

# The Life of Becoming a Buddha Through the Threefold Study

"...practicing with utmost devotion to keep our mind and body perfectly, to know human affairs and universal principles perfectly, and to use our mind and body perfectly,..."

Children learn implicitly from the actions of their parents, but all sages of the three time periods have awakened to the truth of the universe, believing in that truth and, at the same time, adopting it as their teacher. The process of awakening to the truth and instilling it into our mind and body is called "practice based on truth" and "mind-practice."

In this chapter, I have presented a detailed method for instilling the truth into one's mind and body. Each of us has a unique character. These teachings are intended so that we can absorb the truth concretely into our character and discipline ourselves. I hope that you will consider the material in this chapter with reference to your own character.

## "...practice to keep our mind and body perfectly..."

This passage urges us to practice keeping our mind and body perfect and faultless when we use them. In other words, to practice cultivation so that we may maintain the truth self in its original form. We call our original mind the "realm of self-nature" or the "mind-ground." This passage tells us to guard our mind-ground.

This "realm of the mind-ground" refers to a mind state that is ever-calm and ever-alert. The Il-Won-Sang Vow tells us that the Il-Won-Sang Truth is the realm of samādhi beyond all words and speech and the gateway of birth and death that transcends being and nonbeing. Here, "realm of samādhi" and "gateway of birth and death" refer to an ever-calm and ever-alert mind.

In "The Dharma of Timeless Sŏn," the Founding Master called this the mind of true voidness and marvelous existence. He explained that while we have one mind, it is divided into two parts: a mind of true voidness and a mind of marvelous existence.

Depending on the situation, however, it can also be explained in terms of three types. In "The Essential Dharmas of Daily Practice," it is said that the mind-ground is originally free from disturbance, delusion, and wrong-doing. *The Scripture of the Founding Master* refers to a void and complete mind, a right mind, and a precise mind.

Whether he is speaking of two minds or three, he is referring to same one mind.

The pure original mind that all of us possess is something that people lose in the course of their lives. The original mind becomes tainted, obscured by desire, skewed by attachment and greed, and shrouded in dark clouds and fog.

When we fly in an airplane, we travel through the clouds before breaking through to see blue sky stretching out endlessly around us. The minds of us sentient beings are constantly obscured by clouds. Since we can experience neither pleasure nor wisdom when our minds are obscured in this way, this passage tells us to recover that original mind and keep our mind of true voidness and marvelous existence, our ever-calm and ever-alert mind, whenever and wherever we are.

The person who has awakened to the original mind of truth will work hard to preserve the truth. What matters most in guarding our mind and body is that we have a pure mind; for even if we do nothing, temptation will enter from outside and build a house in our minds, beckoning us to live within.

Everyone has preconceptions. We build houses—houses of the people who we love, houses of the people who we hate—and we are forever being eaten away by them. We become slaves to our preconceptions and are rendered incapable of escaping their framework. For this reason, such preconceptions are called "false notions" and "intruding defilements."

The word "intruding" means that they were not with you originally, that they entered from outside.

Because we are filled with these intruding defilements, our original mind loses its luster and we lose our sovereignty. The truth self becomes like a vassal state of intruding defilements, just as Korea spent 36 years as a vassal state of Japan.

We must therefore rid ourselves of intruding defilements. Our truth selves must gain independence. I am referring here to practice to protect this truth self. The great task of practice is to determine how to drive away the dark clouds hanging over the self-nature—the skewed and twisted mind, the noxious weeds of intruding defilements—and create an unsullied mind.

Beginners who are unskilled at practice—and even those who have engaged in a fair bit of practice—need to practice reciting the Buddha's name and uttering incantations. The meaning of the incantation "Na-Mu A-Mi-Ta-Bul" is "to return to one's original mind and rely upon it," while the message of the recitation of the Buddha's name is that we are envisioning our self-buddha.

Once, there were two practitioners who were devoted to practicing by reciting the Buddha's name. They met and talked about their impressions from their study.

One of them said, "I am nothing but the sound of the Buddha's name."

The other practitioner said, "I am nothing but the Buddha's name."

It is said that authentication of having reached a high state was given to the practitioner who said that he was merely the Buddha's name, devoid even of the sound of the recitation.

In *Won*-Buddhism, there is a recitation of the Buddha's name that is performed to recover the buddha in one's self-nature. There is also the Seongju, the "sacred incantation," which we utter to prepare for the next life or to ask for deliverance of the spirit. When we make a wish, we utter the Yeongju, the "spiritual incantation," and we utter the Cheongjeongju, the "purity incantation," when we wish to drive away perverse demons and evil spirits.

If we work hard to learn these incantations, producing the appropriate sounds, the invocations will permeate our minds, and this can provide an occasion for many of the sentient beings who hear them to receive salvation. Through the merits of the incantation, the intruders in our mind and the dark clouds of the five desires will be stripped away layer by layer. In this way, we will take another step toward recovering our original mind.

Next, there is practice for tranquility of the mind. We must practice calming our mind to tranquility through seated meditation in the mornings and evenings, and even during the day when we have no work to do. Master Taesan called this "practice to subdue the mind": calming an excited mind until it is serene.

During the dharma meeting, when we strike the bamboo clapper and say, "Let us enter samādhi," what happens to our mind? At first, it does not linger even for a short samādhi period. It never rests, buzzing with countless thoughts going back and forth. Indeed, it is even more clamorous than it was before we entered samādhi.

However, when we breathe appropriately, settling our minds on the breath, settling our minds on *danjeon*, the elixir field, settling our minds on gentle music, or quietly selecting some object and settling on that, the scattered thoughts disappear. Of course, this does not happen in the space of just one or two days. We practice and practice settling the mind on one place, wherever that may be, so that it becomes a single thought in that place. The single thought deepens until it becomes no mind.

If we exert ourselves in this way, we will learn how to open and close the door of our mind. When we finally shut it tightly, we develop the ability to recover our tranquil self-nature. Thus we are able to guard our original mind.

Next, there is practice to preserve our original nature in the midst of our work. The Founding Master called this the practice of making choices with whole thought. Previously, I talked about practicing to preserve our original nature mainly when we have no work to do. When we engage in practice to preserve our original nature, we focus single-mindedly on the work we are doing. This allows us to work efficiently without separating from our original nature.

When ordinary people work, they are thinking about some other business, experiencing scattered thoughts, greed, and fixation. Because of this, we meet with failure, create bad karma, or develop bad habits. But the practicing person learns to work without leaving the realm of self-nature, practicing while he or she works. This is called "samādhi within action."

Few works of brush calligraphy by the Founding Master survive. There exists one, however, consisting of Chinese characters that reads, "The Same Aspect as the Samādhi, The Same Action as the Samādhi (一相三昧 一行三昧)."

"The Same Aspect as the Samādhi" means "an aspect of the truth remains intact through the practice in which we engage when we are not working." In other words, an ever-calm, ever-alert aspect lingers on. While "The Same Aspect as the Samādhi" refers to the samādhi of preserving one's ever-calm and ever-alert original mind when one is not working, "The Same Action as the Samādhi" means performing the right action for a particular place and time and entering samādhi while one is working, based on a mind that is totally immersed within that work.

There is another expression, "reading samādhi," or "total immersion in reading." "Samādhi in human affairs" is also used to refer to the practice where we achieve one mind during work. This too, is a form of practice in which we create one mind with whatever work we are doing without separating from our self-nature. It serves as a method of practice to guard one's mind.

Among the dharma instructions passed down by Master Chŏngsan to his students, we find the words: "Practice to eliminate our minds at every thought is the practice that we engage in when we are not working. Taking care of matters brightly in everything we do is the practice that we engage in when we have work to do. If we are able to engage in thoughtful practice and practice to eliminate thoughts according to our will, we will learn a great virtue and our mind will grow ever more vast, so that there is no obstruction in anything we do." What this instruction tells us is that we must engage in the great and perfect practice of "one suchness" in action and rest, combining practice in stillness with practice in action.

Among the Zen traditions, we find Tathāgata Zen and Patriarchal Zen. We can imagine a number of different interpretations for this, but it could be argued that Tathāgata Zen is the practice of "The Same Aspect as the Samādhi" during times of rest, and Patriarchal Zen is the practice of "The Same Action as the Samādhi" during times of action.

We can only become truly enlightened when we maintain the same mind in action and rest, and it can only be said to be tathāgata practice when we practice obtaining and using a single mind.

So far, I have been discussing practice to preserve the mind in action and rest, but the body is also important. Cultivation of the mind-nature is important, but so is cultivation of the temperament—that is, cultivating the body. Just as our teeth ache when we have no gums, our minds cannot be properly gathered when our body is weak.

The body that I have in this life is the result of the karmic power that I created in previous lives, and my causal affinity with my parents. So it is that my body contains a soul, which is called "me." The body is a house for the soul, a vessel in which our soul is contained.

If the house of the soul is feeble or flawed, the soul is inevitably affected by this, experiencing greater suffering and uneasiness. Thus, the main actor—the one called "me"—must effectively minister to the body in which it dwells, with a practicing mind. The question is what we need to do to preserve the integrity of all of the functions that the body possesses.

The Founding Master called practice to guard the body "cultivation of temperament." If we minister properly to our bodies, this is half the battle in our practice.

So how do we go about guarding the body? When you go to a mechanic's garage, you see the words, "Wipe it, tighten it, oil it." So it is with our bodies. We must wash ourselves clean for the blood to circulate properly. We must supply ourselves with nutrients, this is similar to oiling the engine, and when necessary, we must take medicine. If we are meticulous about doing this, both the cultivation of temperament and the cultivation of mind-nature will proceed in good order, and our practice will guard both mind and body perfectly. This is something that we truly must do constantly—today, tomorrow, and every day until we grow old and die.

The sages said many things about the mind, but little about the body. For all of our bodily functions to work properly, we must wash our bodies, give them rest, exercise appropriately, and supply the proper nutrition. This training of the body is called "cultivation of temperament."

No matter what courage we may possess in our mind, if our bodily energy is weak we will be oppressed by any wild sensory condition that comes our way, and we will develop fear in our mind. Once we are in the grip of fear, our mind become clamorous, and we end up botching the things we do and making mistakes. This is why discipline of the temperament is so important. If each of us manages our health properly, this will be one way to preserve our body. But there is something that we must be wary of during this process.

The mind must truly become the protagonist and minister properly to the body. If we think only of our health and do whatever the body commands, this has the ultimate outcome of killing the soul. Ministering properly to the body means keeping the soul at peace, attaining buddhahood, and delivering sentient beings.

Ordinary humans and lower-order animals use their mind as their body dictates. If we engage in enough practice, however, our body will operate according to the dictates of the mind. The higher an animal's level, the more the mind comes to govern the body.

We must preserve and train our body, creating one that functions appropriately according to the dictates of the protagonist: the mind. This method of guarding mind and body effectively is called "wholeness of both spirit and flesh" practice.

## "…to know human affairs and universal principles perfectly…"

When you look at me, you see me with your mind. All of us

recognize sights and sounds through the workings of the mind. This functioning of the mind we call "*prajñā* awareness" and "fundamental awareness."

In terms of our original mind, we are no different from the Buddha. The difference lies in whether we can gather that mind and use it in exactly the right way. It is merely a difference of using it when necessary and not using it when it is not necessary, or of using it from a very broad or very narrow perspective. Thus, we must also engage in practice toward gaining the wisdom to make fast and accurate judgments about principles and affairs, making appropriate use of the light of self-nature that each of us possesses.

When our mind is tranquil, there is a light that emerges from it. Our mind has a light of self-nature such that when it is ever-calm, it is also ever-alert. The beginning of the Il-Won-Sang Vow makes reference to the realm of samādhi beyond all words and speech, and when one is in a samādhi state there is also the fundamental spirit of the gateway of birth and death that transcends being and nonbeing.

Our self-nature is one of utter voidness and marvelous existence. "The Dharma of Timeless Sŏn" tells us that when we have utter voidness of the self-nature it is accompanied by the light of marvelous existence. In his *Nanhuajing*, Zhuangzi uses the expression "*xushi shengbai.*" *Xushi* means "empty room"; taken together, the words mean, "Brightness emerges from an empty room."

Long ago, there was a monk who saw a group of monkeys playing. Quietly he said to the monk next to him that each of the monkeys was playing with its own ancient mirror. The other monk responded by asking, "How can you sully something that has no name by calling it 'ancient mirror'?"

Here, "ancient mirror" refers to the fundamental awareness present within all of us.

The Founding Master spoke of the consciousness of heaven and earth. Because heaven and earth have consciousness, he said, we reap soybeans when we plant soybeans, and we reap red beans when we plant red beans. It is this consciousness of heaven and earth that is the light of truth, a self-shining light and spirit that travels with us humans.

The key to inquiry into human affairs and universal principles is to tend carefully to the fundamental spirit present within all of us. This means that we must learn and awaken to the dharma of using that self-shining light. Once we have understood and awakened to this, we will be wise people and achieve the status of the greatly enlightened tathāgata, thus attaining buddhahood.

Thus, it is human affairs and universal principles that we must understand with the fundamental spirit. This entails practice toward understanding everything that must be understood by making appropriate use of the fundamental spirit present within each of us, and the things that must be understood are universal principles and human affairs that are right and wrong, and beneficial and harmful.

### Practice for Understanding and Awakening to Human Affairs

We must engage in practice toward understanding and awakening to human affairs. In human life we are born into work, and we continue working until we die. The person who understands work well is said to be wise, while the person who does not know how to work is said to be incompetent.

The varieties of work are truly numerous. There is edification, the work of transmitting the dharma of the Buddha. The Won-Buddhism order arose in order to carry out this work, and it has since been dedicated to this service. The state, for its part, engages in the "state business" of making the people happy and developing the nation.

Within the home, we find family work. Individuals also engage in their own work. Large and small work, highly worthy work and less worthy work, work that must be done now, work for the future—the varieties are limitless and infinite.

The people who understand work and carry it out effectively and the people who do not understand work and carry it out poorly live together to form societies. When we study the scripture, when we seek mastery of the Way, our ultimate goal is to work well.

The Founding Master said that we must clearly discern between all of the different types of human affairs—determining which are correct, which are mistaken, which are beneficial, and which are harmful—and handle our work in a way that is correct and beneficial. Ordinary humans and sentient beings, however, do more that is mistaken and harmful, leaving the world a noisy and unfortunate place.

One time, I happened to attend a trial at Jeonju District Court. The defendant was a public servant who played cards on Sundays. The prosecutor contended that the man had embezzled the public money that he had had in his pocket, and that he must be sternly punished. This was around the time of the coup on May 16, 1961, and the prosecutor harshly criticized the defendant, saying that he needed to be given an especially heavy sentence because he had gambled in a way unbefitting the status of public servant at a time when the nation needed to establish discipline.

Sitting there in the courtroom, I truly believed that what the prosecutor said was correct.

Some time later, the defendant's attorney made his argument. "There isn't a Korean alive who hasn't gotten caught up playing cards," the attorney said. "When you've caught the fever, you gamble your food away, and you gamble your money away. Pretty soon you can end up gambling with the public money in your pocket. On top of that, he was playing with old friends on Sundays. This was not such a great misdeed. Be lenient with him." Hearing this seasoned attorney's argument, I found myself thinking, this could also be true.

I had heard the prosecutor and believed his argument to be plausible, and I had heard the defense attorney and believed that he was not mistaken, either. I imagined that the judge would have real difficulty making a decision.

Our actions may be well done or poorly done depending on perspective and circumstances, and sometimes poorly done actions are in fact well done actions. It is very difficult to know for sure. When we engage in proper practice with human affairs, we can both advance our society and realize successes at the individual level.

### Practice for Understanding and Awakening to Principles

The next thing we need to understand is principles. We call this "study of the truth." Previously, I spoke about human affairs that are right and wrong, beneficial and harmful. These are social phenomena that arise in the course of a human's life—something akin to natural phenomena.

On the inner side of this conception of human affairs as social phenomenon, there is, by necessity, the truth of principles and actions that are right and wrong, beneficial and harmful, that unfold according to its rules. We must therefore engage in study of the truth in order to understand human affairs fully and precisely. If we wish to go through life performing actions that are beneficial and correct, it is impossible for us to do so if we do not engage in the study of principles.

This world contains within it a world of the sentient and a world of the senseless, and both of these operate according to certain principles. We will find that both the natural world and the world of living creatures are great masses [accumulations] of principles. So when we have mastered principles, we will also have mastered work.

In the broad scheme of things, there is but one principle. All things in this world, both sentient and senseless, are threaded by a single providence. The Founding Master called this single realm the "realm of the great." This is the realm of the Il-Won-Sang principle.

Within the truth, the realm of the absolute, there are a number of different components, each of which has its own distinctive principles. For instance, water has the property of shrinking away, while fire has the property of spreading out. We call the principles of these components the "realm of the small." Within this realm of the phenomenal, these components are ever-changing, never sitting still for a moment.

The Founding Master called this changing realm the "realm of being and nonbeing." With changes from being to nonbeing and vice versa, there is always a hidden principle or rule operating.

We must carry the lantern of self-nature that is the spirit and use it effectively to understand the right and wrong, beneficial and harmful affairs that humans devise, and to understand the principle of great and small, being and nonbeing, that moves this universe and this society.

Now it is time for me to explain the method for achieving understanding and awakening.

### First, We Must Learn About Actions and Principles

Actions and principles are accumulated through all of our studies and experiences. We must learn each individually, from teachers and those with experience. This is why we teach and study history.

For each type of action, there are precursors that come before any action. We must go about learning from these precursors one by one, learn about principles both great and small, and learn about proper and beneficial courses of actions. Also, we must learn about principles and right and wrong actions through personal experience. Throughout our lives, we must maintain the mind of a student who knows how to learn, without concerning ourselves with matters of appearance or age.

Through studying the doctrine, we must learn standards for determining what is right or wrong, beneficial or harmful. Throughout history, humans have studied the scriptures set down by sages. We might say that these scriptures present something akin to standards for human actions and criteria for determining good and evil.

Thus we came to study these scriptures and standards and ultimately codify them into law, creating social principles, ethics, and morals. In the past, religious teachings were a very important element in all societies. Studying these teachings became a way of rising to leadership within a society.

Today, we live in a very different era. In the past, shamans, singers, and theater performers were regarded with contempt. Now, we live in an age in which singers and theatrical performers are afforded special treatment.

Thus we say that there has been a great reversal in the times. The scriptures of the past are standards for the behavior of the past, and so are unsuited to serve as standards for behavior in the world of the future.

We will only be able to become leaders of the future world if we intently study scriptures that present new values and modes of behavior for a new age. And we can only learn anything effectively when we repeatedly rehearse and review what we have learned.

### Next, We Must Engage in Realization Practice with an Inquiring Mind

A person can accumulate a vast store of knowledge by engaging in the kind of practice in which he learns through constantly asking questions of some teacher or leader. However, one does not become enlightened simply through study. We cannot obtain the high level of wisdom characteristic of a sage in this way, nor can we ever free ourselves from evil destinies and samsara. We must engage in realization practice.

Right now, we are engaged in practice toward learning the Il-Won-Sang Vow. In this case, we may believe that we understand, but we may find ourselves forgetting when confronted with reality, or we may be struck dumb when other theorists offer other explanations. It [Enlightenment] cannot become totally ours merely through study. We must awaken to it. When we apply the things we have learned from our dedicated and committed study in our day-to-day life, we inevitably find ourselves asking questions.

Reality differs from what we understand, and we find ourselves asking, "Why should that be?" When we commit ourselves to answering these questions, we will experience the truly great joy of awakening—the "aha!" moment.

The Founding Master had questions about the sky and the clouds. He saw his own parents being tender with each other and the couple next door fighting, and he asked, "Why should that be?" He harbored profound questions about the universe, nature, and life, and decided to consult with a mountain spirit and a teacher to understand these things. But in the end he was unable to understand them.

All of these questions came together as one big question for him: "What am I to do about this in the future?" The day he answered that question is the day we now recognize as The Great Enlightenment and Founding Day. Thus, the Founding Master said that questioning is the key to great enlightenment.

As we go about living our lives, we encounter a great many things that we cannot understand. Similarly, when we study *Won-Buddhism* we also find that we cannot understand many of the things that are said. When we encounter some statement that we cannot understand in common sense terms, we should not simply let it be. We should insist on studying first, and if we still do not understand after our study, we should regard it as a critical phrase, and focus our practice on solving it.

Master Taesan said that if a practitioner has no questions in his notebook, he is not a true practitioner. We must extract questions one at a time from the everyday life that is closest to us. The exalted questions that are never even asked do not weigh on our minds in any real sense, and so there is no way to answer them. They merely make our heads hurt. We must proceed persistently, beginning with the questions that are weighing on our minds. When I contrast the things that I fervently believe with reality, the disparity between them sometimes leaves me harboring profound questions. Questions can also arise out of profound attention to our work or to the scriptures. Other times, a teacher may give us the right question.

If we carry that question with us, studying it intently when our head is clear, letting it go and then inquiring intensely once again, repeating this process over and over, there will come a day when the fog lifts and we see the road ahead of us.

Once, there was a *kyomu* who went to pay respects to a teacher. "How old are you?" the teacher asked, to which the younger man replied with his physical age.

"No, no," the teacher said. "How old is your mind?" The *kyomu* was left speechless, unable to answer. That question— what was his mind's age?—was driven into his heart like a nail, and he thought about the matter deeply before finally coming to a realization.

What about you? How old is your soul? I do not mean your body. Our scriptures contain twenty "Essential Cases for Questioning." If you read them reverentially, or if you read "The Principle of the Nature," "Doctrine," and other sections in *The Scripture of the Founding Master*, you will find yourself with questions about principles.

Once we have questions, we should work to learn and understand. In the course of our search, we will discover things that we do not understand no matter how much we study. If we incubate them as a hen does an egg, there will be an awakening.

### Practice for Appraising Our Realizations

As our practice deepens, the possibility presents itself that we may become arrogant as we gain enlightenment and understanding. We often see those people who noisily proclaim their realization to the world.

A few years back, stories about the "rapture" were all over the newspapers. They said that someone who believed in a particular religion and prayed would be saved and ascend to Heaven. The world was shocked when the appointed time for the rapture came and no one ascended to Heaven—leaving these people looking like fools.

Cases like this are not simply about people being taken in by the preposterous claims of a religious leader. They did have a realization in some spiritual sense, but it was a mistaken realization. Among the different types of mistaken realizations, we find misapprehensions, misguided thinking, and misperceptions. It is a matter of faulty realization. We have a bias in our perceptions, where we realize only one aspect of things. In such cases, we have awakened to only a part, but are convinced that we have awakened to the whole. So when we have realized something, the first thing we must do is to take it to a teacher for appraisal.

Buddhists call this "authentication." If this process is neglected, we are liable to suffer major frustration. In the larger world, we are given some kind of certification—a graduation diploma, for example—when we complete the appropriate coursework. The purpose of this is to set right what is mistaken.

If there is something that we understand for certain within the principles of great and small, being and nonbeing, or work that is right and wrong, beneficial and harmful, we must put it into practice in our daily lives. When we go about embodying what we have understood and awakened to in depth and breadth within our daily lives, we may sense inadequacies in our realization. In this case, we repeat the process of broadening and deepening our realization.

At first, we awaken to the original nature of the mind and the fact that we and the universe are not divided. Next, we discover the principle of retribution and response of cause and effect within our minds, and we awaken to the principle of alternating predominance of *yin* and *yang* within the universe. We awaken to the fact that all things are intertwined through cause and effect, and we come to predict how things will unfold in the future based on what we see in the present. We discover small realizations all coming together into one great enlightenment.

## "…and to use our mind and body perfectly…"

Our body and mind are suffused with marvelous creative

transformations. Our compassion for someone who is poor, the shame we feel after committing a misdeed, our desire to repay a debt of gratitude, our desire to rest after vigorous exercise, our desire to move again after we rest—all of these are the workings of the Il-Won Truth. When the universe changes through formation, subsistence, decay, and emptiness and through spring, summer, autumn, and winter, and when all things change through birth, old age, sickness, and death, all of this is the profound working of the truth. When the truth operates, it does so in a way suited to that particular time and place. We sentient beings engage in practice toward using our mind and body perfectly by awakening to the Il-Won-Sang Truth and substituting the creative transformations of the truth for those of our body and mind.

The Founding Master used the term "Choice in Action" to refer to a practice dedicated to using our mind and body perfectly. This means that practice involves boldly doing that which must be done, and boldly abandoning that which must be abandoned. Once we use our mind and body properly, blessings and virtue will accumulate, and we will be filled with the happy feeling of ultimate bliss.

Though there may be realizations that come from gaining powers of cultivation through Cultivating the Spirit as well as powers of inquiry, that cultivation and inquiry will have no real effect if we do not put them into practice in our daily lives. Thus, the practice of Choice in Action could be called the flower, the product, and the goal of the Threefold Study.

## The Need to Instill Good Habits

The practice of using our mind and body perfectly first involves breaking our bad habits and instilling good ones.

Each of us has certain habits of the mind: habits of resentment, habits of fancy, habits of anxiety—these are the habits of the sentient being. They ultimately manifest themselves in actions, and so we commit misdeeds.

We also have habits of speech. Some people have good minds, but their words are coarse. Habits of speech can cause fissures between ourselves and others and breed resentments.

Next, there are habits of the body. Our manners are about the way we move our body, and if our habits are unsophisticated, uncultivated, or uncouth, this can lead others to underestimate us.

We must commit ourselves sincerely to discovering these mistaken habits characteristic of sentient beings and to correct them one by one.

"The Essential Dharmas of Daily Practice" could be characterized as a standard for instilling good habits, while "The Essential Discourse on Commanding the Nature" and "The Precepts" provide examples that lead us to use mind and body with the habits of a buddha-bodhisattva.

Only by practicing proper habits and utterly abandoning improper ones—no matter how comfortable and appealing we may find them—do we engage in the practice of Choice in Action. All ordinary humans and sentient beings possess sentient being habits that they picked up during their countless previous lives. We call this "personality" or "individuality." If we have habits that are not helpful to society's or our own development, habits that block the road ahead of us and go against the moral code of society, then we must ferret each of them out and put our heart and soul into fixing them. Bad habits become instilled without our knowledge, and it is very difficult to break them. But we have no choice. We must break them for our own sake, for our family's sake, and for our community's sake. We develop habits thoughtlessly, thinking little of them, and this becomes a trap for us, preventing us from ever being free. Breaking those bad habits is a shortcut to attaining buddhahood.

Our mind foundation is tranquil by nature, wise by nature, harmonious and virtuous and righteous by nature. If we wish to make the proper choices in our actions, we must first recover the harmony that is a natural part of our minds and the precepts of free-from-error self-nature, and use a mind that is free of error at every time and in every place.

The Il-Won Truth that governs this universe with its limitless power of creative transformation functions as a creator that carries the universe through changes of formation, subsistence, decay, and emptiness, and of spring, summer, autumn, and winter; carries objects through the changes of birth, old age, sickness, and death; causes the winds, cloud, rain, dew, frost, and snow; and causes all objects to grow and bear fruit according to their characteristics. In the Il-Won-Sang Vow, this is called the gateway of birth and death that transcends being and nonbeing.

### The Need to Put Our Judgment into Practice

In the proper sequence for practice, we must first make clear judgments about human affairs and universal principles with a mind free of delusion and turbulence. Forming a judgment before putting something into practice is like creating a blueprint before building a house. If we have a good blueprint, we will build a good house. In everything we do, we must first complete our blueprint, and only afterwards begin construction. Proceeding straight into action without first forming a clear judgment is an exceedingly foolish and dangerous thing to do. Thus if we think first about whatever we are doing and put it into practice with the use of mind and body in our immediate reality, this is what we call choice in action that is free of error. In many cases, however, our judgments are unclear, and we behave according to habit or circumstance in our practice. We must therefore make sure that we form a precise judgment beforehand and follow that judgment in our actions.

For example, we know for certain that if we are walking along and find a muddy stream in front of us, we must avoid it. This judgment is put into practice without any need for hesitation. Such a state is called "sudden cultivation upon sudden enlightenment."

Those who are still unskilled with their practice must work hard, first of all when using mind and body to engage in Inquiry into Human Affairs and Universal Principles, and then make certain of their judgment and use it as a kind of compass or blueprint for their practice. When we form a judgment but fail to put it into practice due to old habits or excessive desire, it is as though we are issuing a bad check.

The Founding Master instructed us to do what we know is right even at risk of our life. Ordinary humans, however, seem to keep their judgments and practice separate. We must form judgments that we can put into practice, and when we have formed a judgment we must have the will to put it into practice.

In our experiences with different people we find that there are some who think well, yet those thoughts are not put into practice when they run up against the reality. We call a person like this an "idea man." This resembles nothing more than a beautiful flower that has failed to blossom and it is incapable of bringing about any special virtue, but even such people can gradually come to form realistic, reliable judgments if they commit themselves fully to putting their judgments into practice.

**The Need to Use Mind and Body According to Circumstances**

Even when we have made the right judgment, the possibility exists that the circumstances will be different on the ground. This requires that we modify our previous judgment and form a new one. In such cases, it could be said that the choice is now at a higher level. It is therefore important that we practice in a way suited to that particular time and place, regardless of any ideas we may have prepared beforehand. This is called "middle way action" or "action in time."

The ideal capability, and the most effective form of action, is the appropriate use of body and mind in a way suited to that particular time and place. This could be termed something like "flexible practice."

Consider a football match. The first thing the coach does is to examine the opposing team's tactical plan. He establishes his own plan to penetrate it and trains the athletes in the appropriate tactics. However, the other team's plans may be different once the match actually begins. In such cases, it becomes necessary to shift rapidly away from the planned tactics.

If the car we are driving is jerking at every stop and start, people say that we do not know how to drive. When someone is a good driver, we do not know when that person has started or stopped. In the same way, a higher level of choice in action only emerges when we engage in this action in time, mindful of seamlessly removing the traces of halting and continuation in order to increase our resourcefulness when we are choosing actions with body and mind.

Once we have gained enough practice with resourceful choice in action, our energy and mind reach an accord, giving us the power to regulate our energy as we wish. When we regulate our mind, we gain the ability to regulate the energy of other people. If we work constantly to correct habits of mind and body, put our judgments into practice, and engage in middle way practice suited to whatever time and place in which we find ourselves, we will operate like the truth. The key practice that serves as the cornerstone to this Choice in Action practice is the assessment of mindfulness and unmindfulness. I believe that it is only possible for someone to be sacred if that person has had the experience of practicing mindfulness hundreds of millions of times.

What enables us to correct our habits, put our thoughts into practice, and engage in middle way action is the spirit of practice. This is what we call "mindfulness practice."

Changes in heaven and earth proceed naturally and automatically. Previously, this was referred to as the "gateway of birth and death that transcends being and nonbeing." With the gateway to our minds, the mind emerges when we encounter a sensory condition, and it may change to another mind or go away completely when the condition passes.

Thoughts change according to a process of arising, abiding, transforming, and ceasing. The mind changes based on this process, and nature becomes the gateway of birth and death naturally and automatically. With our mind, however, it is impossible to open and close the gateway of birth and death simply according to our wishes. It is crucial that we train ourselves and engage in Choice in Action practice toward opening and closing our mind.

We are capable of thinking and not thinking. The gateway to the mind can be adjusted like the aperture on a camera. When we reach the point where we can do this freely, dharma power emerges, we become sages, and we are able to unite with the universe.

Thus the practitioners who have chosen the path of practice close the doors of their mind tightly so that no thought can enter, and they know how to open and close the mind so that the thoughts inside do not escape to the outside. This is what we call the mind's choice in action. We gain training experience with this through assessment of the mindful and unmindful—the foundation of Choice in Action practice.

When we use mind and body properly, we can use our mind as we wish and use our body as we wish. Sentient beings are tormented by their bodies. They suffer because they are unable to control the desires that arise in their minds. The body and mind become places of torment.

If, however, we cultivate the Way properly and use body and mind well, we create ultimate bliss in our mind and rejoice in an unparalleled bliss of mind. We create a paradise with our body, so that the body is truly a good house.

If we use body and mind properly, they become instruments for creating blessings, and we can go about bringing peace to the world and making eternal lives of abundant blessings and wisdom.

Previously, we considered methods for engaging in Cultivating the Spirit practice to guard mind and body, practice with Inquiry into Human Affairs and Universal Principles, and Choice in Action practice for use of mind and body. We see people who focus primarily on Cultivating the Spirit, engaging only in practice toward giving an impression of stability and purity. Others focus on inquiry practice and possess only knowledge or wisdom. Still others focus on Choice in Action practice, so that it is only their capabilities and know-how that are strong. When someone focuses on only one aspect of practice, it is natural for character flaws to emerge. It is similar to the way in which we develop malnutrition and become ill if we do not have a balanced diet. Just as we must eat balanced portions of food from different sources, so too it is very misguided for us to focus on only one area of mind-practice or to believe that any one area is more important than the others.

The Il-Won-Sang Truth has three qualities. There is the aspect of void and calm, the aspect of light, and the harmonious aspect.

We must emulate all of these aspects perfectly; if we emulate only one element of the Il-Won-Sang, we will become someone who does not truly understand the Il-Won-Sang Truth. It could be described as something akin to the biased affections of a child who thinks only of his father and ignores the contributions of his mother.

One of the things about which the Founding Master was very wary was the practitioner who engages only in cultivation and neglects putting judgment into practice, who engages only in inquiry and lacks cultivation, or who values only putting judgment into practice and has deficiencies in inquiry. He said that such a person was "only a partial person of the Way," and cautioned that this is a highly mistaken form of practice. We must carry out all three elements of the Threefold Study practice—cultivation, inquiry, and choice—so that we may become imbued with a character that is perfect like the Il-Won-Sang.

 Chapter Six

# THE LIFE OF PROGRESSION AND GRACE

"…with utmost devotion…so that, by progressing rather than regressing and receiving grace rather than harm,…"

The meaning of this part of the vow is that we should regard the Dharmakāya Buddha Il-Won-Sang as the object of our faith and the model for our practice, committing ourselves to the Dharmakāya Fourfold Grace faith and Threefold Study practice with utmost devotion so that our character and dharma rank progress. It means that we must receive the Fourfold Grace and not allow our character and dharma rank to regress; that we must cultivate our buddha capabilities by ensuring that we do not receive harm from the Fourfold Grace; and that we should tame our actions into a life that is a constant source of grace in our relationship with others and ensure that we do not allow our character to degenerate and that we do not receive harm from others.

## "…with utmost devotion …"

In our lives, there is nothing more important than sincerity. Sincere committment means constant repetition with a sound mind. Only when we are repeating constantly, with a sound mind, is our committment truly sincere. When we have all of these things— exclusive dedication and exertion, right standards, and unlimited repetition—we have what is considered utmost devotion.

A student once asked his teacher, "What is the single most important word in this world?" Immediately, the teacher responded by writing the word "sincerity (誠)." "'Sincerity' is the most important word," the teacher said. "Commit yourself sincerely in everything you do."

The *Doctrine of the Mean* says, "Without sincerity, there is nothing." Without sincere commitment, nothing can exist and no ventures can succeed.

If we are to commit ourselves sincerely, we must have a standard. Without a standard, there can be no commitment, and the sincerity will not be sustained.

That standard is the Il-Won-Sang faith and practice of the Threefold Study. We must adopt four standards: one for requiting the Fourfold Grace, one for Cultivating the Spirit, one for Inquiry into Human Affairs and Universal Principles, and one for Choice in Action.

Every one of us has had the experience of making a firm resolution, only to see it last a mere three days. Sincere commitment means repeating these three-day resolutions over and over again, stringing them together until they last a lifetime. In other words, we must engage in constant repetition based on a standard.

They say that a heavyweight boxer has the power of a four-ton truck in his fists. The release of such power from such a small fist is possible because of repeated practice.

We, too, can generate the same kind of power through constant repetition of bright and clear and warm actions based on the standard of the Threefold Study. When we are repeating these actions, they will produce no great effect if we do so without thinking or while thinking other thoughts. We must engage in repetition with one mind. When we are sincere in our commitment, we gain strength and awesome power.

There is something magical that you feel when you see a practitioner of Chinese medicine at work. The dosage is written on the prescription, but even when the practitioner merely picks up the ingredients with his fingers without weighing them on the scale, they are exactly the right amount.

A magical harmony has arisen over the course of constant repetitions. Our mothers, too, could apply a dash of salt while preparing our meals and find exactly the right degree of saltiness. This is all the result of sincere commitment.

If you pray wholeheartedly and practice the Threefold Study with utmost sincerity, you will gradually acquire the ability to see into the future, as well as both inner mental powers and outward powers of influence, allowing you to leave a deep impression on others.

Typically, we dedicate ourselves sincerely to only those things that we can see and touch. We must realize that if we begin now to give our sincere commitment to a mind that is unseen and unknowable, and to the Il-Won-Sang Truth that governs the universe, the awesome powers that result will be far greater and come much faster.

## The Life of Progression

"Progression" means that if we sincerely commit ourselves to faith and practice, our character and dharma power will improve.

If we practice the Threefold Study, we will be reborn with

a character of freedom, wisdom, and mercy. Our life will be transformed from an empty one obscured by desires into a life of truth, and we will become sages. This is what is meant by progression.

Among the societies in which people live, we see a great variety of different ways of life. Some people are living worthwhile lives, others are not, and we can categorize these lives according to the worlds of the six destinies.

Those living the lives of denizens of hell wander hopelessly amid sickness and pain. To such people, the delivering hand of a sage is far away indeed. There are also people who fixate solely on eating, like hungry ghosts, and on combativeness, sparing no thought for ethics and morality or consideration for any thing or person besides their own desires.

Those living the lives of animals give themselves over to a filthy and dissolute life without manners or shame, indulging in carnal desires and indolence. Others live the lives of asuras: ever roaming and without order, lacking any center in the things they do, skewed only in one direction.

Those living the lives of human beings have both desirous minds and virtuous minds, alternating between joy and pain, and entertain either the mind of the Way or an unwholesome mind depending on the circumstances. Among human beings, we find those of the topmost stratum who are educated and see themselves as living a conscientious life. This is the class of religious workers and buddha-bodhisattvas—practitioners of the Way who live heavenly lives, experience simple desires, enjoy performing acts of charity, live according to the mind of the Way, and never fail to engage in penitence. Of course, if a person living as a human adopts the mind of one of the other five destinies for too long, his habits and dharma power from this lifetime may result in regression in the next: the sentient being who lived the life of a denizen of hell may be born into actual hell, while the person who lived the life of the asura may fail to receive a body and instead roam about as a ghost.

As stated before, when we commit ourselves sincerely to a life of faith and cultivation of the Way, we will progress from an animal's life to the life of a human, or from a human being's life to the life of a heavenly being.

There is one Won-Buddhist who previously lived the life of a hungry ghost. So severe was it that he was ostracized in his home and neighborhood for being a good-for-nothing. After a decade or so of Won-Buddhism mind-practice, which he entered thanks to a causal affinity with a kyomu, the change was so great that other believers and the people in his neighborhood lauded him as having become an enlightened one. Of course, we still have to wait and see, but it may be that he has progressed several levels, from asura to heavenly being.

Among the ordinary grade believers who have taken refuge in *Won*-Buddhism, entered the order, and received dharma names, we find people from every class imaginable. There are people who have lived the lives of denizens of hell, those who have been requited with the asura destiny and lived a life of roaming, and those who have always enjoyed heavenly bliss like that of an enlightened one, living a blameless life.

If these believers, from their different classes, carry out the four duties of morning and evening mental affirmation, helping others, observance of regulations, and guidance of people to the *Won*-Buddhist faith, and if they engage in mind-practice for many decades, they will ultimately progress to the grade of special faith, the grade of the battle between dharma and Māra, the status of Māra defeated, the status of beyond the household, and the status of tathāgata.

Imagine what a great life these ordinary human beings will lead as they cycle through the six destinies if they progress to the level of buddha-bodhisattva, meeting a teacher of this order and freely taking charge of the six destinies, coming and going as they please.

Whenever I find in my practice that I have developed a lazy mind and begun to feel resentful of others, I repeat the words of one of our hymns: "It is difficult to become a human, yet I have already become one. It is difficult to hear the buddhadharma, yet I am already hearing it. If my body cannot be delivered in this life, then what life must I wait for until it can be delivered?" When I do so, I experience my mind coming to life, and a mind of exertion arising. Let us all exert ourselves and accumulate good works so that we proceed along the road of progression.

## The Life of Regression

Regression is when our humanity deteriorates, when we go astray, when our faith and our practice lapse indefinitely.

Sometimes, in the midst of committed *Won*-Buddhism practice with a special sense of faith, our environment suddenly improves or deteriorates, and we are unable to continue practicing and performing works. When this happens, we end up regressing.

Other times in the course of our practice with the battle between dharma and Māra, we gain an understanding or are recognized by others and develop a feeling of arrogance. We come to think lightly of our teacher or *kyomu*. When this happens, our mind is gradually corrupted, laziness emerges, and we regress.

It is said it becomes ever more difficult to receive salvation when we go astray after engaging in practice with the battle between dharma and Māra. Many times we seek the cause of regression and degeneration in others. There may be factors such as our workplace situation or family circumstances, but we must understand that problems of the mind and the self are greater.

In order to avoid regression, we must establish a firm sense of faith. The greatest cause of regression is when our faith is weak and incorrect. The next greatest cause is greed. All things grow through gradual changes according to a sequence. The same is true for practice and faith: they proceed from small to large, but when we practice and perform works with a spirit of greed, we may become impatient. If things fail to live up to our hopes, we feel frustrated and give up, and we end up regressing.

The next thing we must be wary of is laziness. All of us are given to indolence, to seeking out comfort. Our bodies, in particular, have an ever-present desire for comfort. Cultivation of the Way demands a very sincere commitment, and if we allow ourselves to be hindered by indolence and put things off until the next day we will wind up a perennial regressor, forever confined to that place.

After that, we must be wary of delusion. Living an effective life of faith and cultivation of the Way requires wisdom. If we pursue it foolishly, without any know-how, we will end up regressing.

At school, we find some people who fail to graduate and end up having to repeat a year. The shame that they experience is truly indescribable. If a person who is very wealthy and is used to traveling everywhere by taxi suddenly loses all his money and is forced to walk everywhere, the sorrow will be truly difficult to bear.

While the person who strives, even after regressing, can rise up once again, the person who has given up and is hopelessly resigned to regression will go from regression to regression, from hardship to greater hardship. It is a truly sad sight to behold.

In Bojo's *Secrets on Cultivating the Mind*, it says that an ordinary human encountering the buddhadharma is like a blind turtle encountering a piece of driftwood. For a blind turtle to survive out in the ocean, it needs to find a branch when it surfaces so that it can sit on top and breathe. But it is not easy to find drifting branches in a vast ocean, and even if one happens to float by, it is very difficult for a blind turtle to climb on top.

All of you here have found the correct dharma. You must believe truly in this buddhadharma, devote yourselves to your teachers' teachings, learn from them, and practice on your own. You must progress, not regress.

## "…receiving grace…"

When we act, we necessarily affect other people and objects either directly or indirectly. If our influence is positive, the fruits of grace will come to us. If we do something bad, we will reap the fruits of harm from others in the distant future. Thus, we should make buddha offerings for everyone we encounter and ensure that we receive grace.

When we are facing difficult and trying times, when we are having difficulty making a decision, when our minds are restless and obscured by desire, when we have become arrogant about things we have done well, we must put our palms together before the Dharmakāya Buddha and offer a mental affirmation and formal prayer. Additionaly, if we abide by the precepts, empty our minds through seated meditation practice and timeless Sŏn practice, awaken to cause and effect by studying the scriptures every chance we get, open our eyes to the principle of the nature, and engage in many years of practice with the Threefold Study so that we become aware of human affairs, we will progress as individuals.

The progressing person naturally gives off a bright, clear, and warm energy all around, and when we follow a life of mental affirmation and formal prayer, an auspicious energy will be transmitted to the causal affinities around us and the affinities of those affinities.

Just as television is broadcast and telephone calls are transmitted through wavelengths of electricity, so a wavelength of grace propagates from the person who is progressing. The hidden help and hidden virtue of the Dharmakāya Buddha

Fourfold Grace appear, and the gateway of grace opens up ahead of the progressing person, thanks in part to the earnest attention of his teachers.

Ordinary people do not know who is giving them blessings and happiness. They have a vague belief that it is the result of good luck or the stars, or perhaps their ancestors. The life of the ordinary person is thus a mass of contradictions, and it could be said that they are living very pathetic lives indeed, lives of merely wishing for a stroke of good fortune.

Each person has his own destiny and past lives. Sometimes blessings and happiness happen to come his way, and sometimes ill fortune visits him unexpectedly. Who exactly is giving him these blessings, this happiness, these catastrophes?

Only when we know this for certain can we be said to have acquired the wisdom of the truth. The disasters that befall us and the blessings and happiness that happen to come our way are not the result of our tending well to the ancestral grave site, nor do they result from our having a propitious site for our home. Nor indeed do they come from an unfair god who deals blessings to us and disasters to others.

As is explained at the very beginning of the Il-Won-Sang Vow, the realm that transcends being and nonbeing—the Il-Won-Sang Truth that transcends all questions of fondness or contempt, being or nonbeing—deals out catastrophes or blessings and happiness with utter impartiality and selflessness according to a person's mental and bodily functioning.

This is why we talk about receiving what we create for ourselves. If we do good to others, the Il-Won-Sang Truth gives us blessings and happiness, and if we do harm to others the Il-Won-Sang truth-buddha will not fail to bring us harm.

When we give something to somebody, that person gives back to us. We do not give to the person in the south and receive from the person in the north. We must have firm belief in the principle of reaping as we sow and work diligently to accumulate acts of charity and good works through spirit, body, and material things for all people and all living creatures around us.

Those acts of charity and good work become the blessings that we receive in this life or the next. We must awaken to the principle of retribution and response of cause and effect, reaping as we sow with every individual. We must understand what that person wants and how we can help him progress, and generate grace effectively by performing a buddha offering suited to him.

If he commits a misdeed against us in this life, we must accept it as requital for a debt from a previous life. Indeed, if we help him, the harm will be converted into grace.

We are familiar with the figure of Huineng. One evening, he was trying to go to sleep, and he detected a strange blood lust. He contemplated his past affairs and realized that in a past life he had failed to repay a debt of ten lings of silver. He saw that someone was now coming to reclaim the debt. Huineng hid the ten lings of silver under his mat and took cover. During the night, the assassin came. He saw that it was another monk named Xingchang.

Huineng came out of hiding and said, "I failed to repay a debt of ten lings of silver in a previous life, but it is not worth dying at your hand. Take the coins and go."

After that, the story goes, Xingchang reflected deeply before finally becoming a special student of Huineng and putting his gratitude into practice.

Fundamentally, if we gain the three great powers of the Threefold Study and possess a warm virtuousness in our hearts and a constant spirit of serving the public, our words and deeds will ever be those of generous mercy in both mind and body, but our acts of charity and merit will only be great—will only be eternal grace—when we perform them without leaving any sign that we have done so.

## "…rather than harm …"

The person who is regressing and heading astray is certain to be treated poorly and scornfully and to receive no aid from those around him. Harm is the disaster that happens to come our way.

Nature, heaven and earth, our parents, our fellow beings, and laws afford us unlimited grace, but whereas the progressing person simply receives this grace as it is, the regressing and ungrateful person receives grace as harm.

When we were children, things like honey and taffy were delicious treats. The progressing person has self-control and can measure the effects of the honey against him, consuming it in appropriate amounts for its health benefits.

The regressing person lacks self-control and eats indiscriminately without understanding the proper way to use honey. Thus honey affords the same sweet grace to the progressing person and the regressing person alike, but the progressing person uses it graciously, in a way that is helpful to his life, while the regressing person uses it to excess and receives harm.

All organisms are imbued with a unique energy according to the functioning of their mind. When that energy is strong, it transforms into a wave that ripples out to the people around them. People who are progressing generally send out waves of grace, causing a beneficial ripple effect in other people and organizations. The people and objects that encounter these waves of grace respond in kind with their own waves of grace.

Thus the progressing person is a person who receives grace. The regressing person, in contrast, has a constant malicious desire to harm others, and so he naturally comes to exude waves of harm to those around him. When this happens, he becomes isolated as a matter of course, and those who receive his waves of harm ultimately retaliate against him. Thus the regressing person is punished, going from suffering to worse suffering.

Our six sense organs—the eyes, ears, nose, tongue, body, and mind—can be instruments for creating grace or instruments for creating harm. Our faith and practice are therefore about turning those organs into instruments for creating grace. This is exertion and Sŏn.

If we make buddha offerings to others with sense organs that produce grace, it stands to reason that grace will return to us. Conversely, if we choose to use the precious instruments of our body, mouth, and mind in a way that creates harm, whether this is out of greed, fixation, or bad habit, the ones who experience that harm, unless they are buddhas, will inevitably respond in kind with harm. This requital is a creative transformation belonging to the gateway of birth and death that transcends being and nonbeing.

Fortunately, we have learned the path of progression, and we have learned to fear regression. We must awaken and resolve ourselves to produce grace with our six sense organs, and not to bring misfortune and regression upon ourselves by producing harm.

# Chapter Seven

# THE RESULT OF COMPLETING OUR VOW

> "...we deluded beings make this vow so that...
> we may attain the awesome power of Il-Won and
> be unified with the substance and nature of Il-Won."

When we make a vow to attain the limitless, awesome power of the Il-Won-Sang Truth and put this vow into practice, and when we make a vow to actually become the Il-Won-Sang Truth and put that into practice, we become a tathāgata of the great, perfect, and right enlightenment. This is the completion of our vow.

Attaining the awesome power of Il-Won and being unified with its substance and nature represent the state of the buddha who has experienced great enlightenment of the Dharmakāya Buddha Il-Won-Sang Truth and become unified with the Il-Won-Sang Truth. Unification with the substance and nature is the state of the tathāgata who completely owns the Il-Won-Sang Truth, and attainment of the awesome power of Il-Won means that the power of the Fourfold Grace is always with the tathāgata who has unified with the substance and nature.

When we progress and progress still further, we are said to unify with the substance and nature of Il-Won-Sang. If we receive grace and continue receiving grace, we are said to attain the awesome power of Il-Won-Sang. This is called the ultimate vow, a vow that causes the Il-Won-Sang to become our own.

## "…attain the awesome power of Il-Won …"

The universe is truly vast, heaven and earth truly eternal. Together, they represent an incredibly long eon. There is a master who governs this heaven and earth. That master is called the Il-Won-Sang Truth.

This truth possesses myriad creative transformations and awesome power. It carries the power to transform the universe through formation, subsistence, decay, and emptiness, and the limitless creative transformations and power to make all things progress and regress through birth, old age, sickness, and death according to the mental and bodily functioning of the four types of birth.

How much does this Earth weigh? How heavy is the moon? That massive moon circles the Earth once every month. The Earth revolves on its own axis while also orbiting around the sun. What a tremendous force the Earth must possess!

A few times each year we marvel at the awesome power of typhoons. At the same time, we gape at how much greater the power of nature is than that of humans. Where does this awesome power of nature come from? Who makes it that way?

All the myriad things in this world possess their own forms and colors. The truth makes the right fruit blossom for each seed and allows things that are different from that seed to live together in harmony. It punishes the person who has transgressed and rewards the person who has created good karma.

This is the wisdom and grace of the truth. It is a truth-buddha that possesses such creative transformations and capabilities. In short, the unlimited gracious workings of the truth are its awesome power.

All sentient beings live within the grace of that awesome power. They are simply unaware of this, but because of their ignorance of the grace and power of the truth, ordinary humans and sentient beings are ungrateful, and they receive punishment for their ingratitude.

If we awaken to the Il-Won-Sang Truth and practice the realm of samādhi, in which our mind is free from perverse states of mind and scattered thoughts, and awaken to the gateway of birth and death that transcends being and nonbeing, we can gain the dharma power of one who is not divided from the Il-Won-Sang, living our lives with the unlimited and awesome power of the truth.

Humans cannot live by their powers alone. Our lives are far more powerful when there is something to serve as our backing. It was once said that "we must at least draw upon the energy of the ridge between rice fields." In the old days, money came from agriculture, so in today's language we might say that you need money to live.

If a family member is appointed to a high government post, that family is said to have cause for celebration. When there is a government official in your family, your influence improves and you gain power.

In human society, "power" refers to things such as economic might and privileges, but when we awaken to the truth and engage in true requital of grace, we gain the tremendous might of the truth. Thus it could be said that the power of the buddha-bodhisattva is a fearsome force like that of heaven and earth.

Ordinary people must have solid collateral to borrow money

from the bank, but when someone has solid credit, that person can borrow a lot of money without necessarily having to put anything up for collateral.

The truth is the same way. To the practitioners who are utterly committed to requiting the Fourfold Grace and to upholding their pledge with mental affirmation and formal prayer, the truth confers the awesome might of its grace. How could it not, when we live a life of great faith, practice the Threefold Study appropriately, perform proper requital of grace, and make proper buddha offerings?

Awesome might is the grace afforded us by those around us: our parents, our teachers, our fellow beings. For instance, I know of someone who is strangely blessed with innate virtue. Despite having no capital to speak of, this person does well through the help of others. This is what is meant by "awesome power."

It is not only humans who live in this world. There are also heavenly beings and asuras, and it is said that in some cases they help practitioners who are especially committed to their practice and their life of faith. These cases, as well, could be described as a kind of awesome power.

When buddha-bodhisattvas establish some power of aspiration, speak to others to achieve that aspiration, and offer their prayers, the Dharmakāya Buddha Fourfold Grace aids them and displays the wondrous and awesome power to make it so. In such cases, ordinary people say that luck was with them, that something they expected to fail succeeded. Of course, there may be an element of fortune, but it is really the awesome power of the Fourfold Grace of Heaven and Earth, Parents, Fellow Beings, and Laws.

Beginning three years before the 1988 Seoul Olympic Games, Master Taesan delivered many dharma instructions in which he spoke of going "beyond the walls of tribalism, beyond the walls of the state, beyond the walls of religion." He said that peace would only come when ours is a world where there is free movement in all three areas. Strangely enough, the theme of the 1988 Olympics ended up being "breaking down the walls."

"Going beyond the walls" and "breaking down the walls" are very similar in meaning, so it was quite astonishing when the theme of the Games was announced.

It is said that the person who engages in deep truth-practice possesses the power of heaven. In other words, such a one possesses creative transformations of truth that are like heaven itself. A person who is elected president assumes total authority for the government. In the same way, one who becomes a presiding buddha for the age and engages in profound practice acquires remarkable power like the truth.

The miracle of the seal of blood occurred when the nine senior disciples of *Won*-Buddhism prayed with utmost sincerity and the spirit of "Sacrifice with No Regret." But because sages must provide an example for sentient beings, they mainly use the creative transformations and awesome power of nature rather than unnatural miracles.

People who have engaged in mind-practice and made the truth their own have a truly tremendous power to move people, one that allows them to command the minds of others as they wish. This is the awesome power of mercy. Buddha-bodhisattvas are filled with the spirit of reverence to the buddha—free from perverse thoughts, free from the selfish desire to serve themselves, and interested in knowing what they must do to help others. The minds of those who come to meet these buddha-bodhisattvas melt away, so that it becomes an embodiment of that unlimited influence.

During his long struggle with illness, Master Chŏngsan heard that some of his students were offering a special prayer for his recovery. "You do not have to say any more prayers," he said, "for I am someone known to the dharma realm, and the dharma realm will decide my life or death as it sees fit."

Could an ordinary human say that he is someone known to the dharma realm? I am certain that Master Chŏngsan, someone who possessed an awesome power like that of heaven and earth, would himself have said that the dharma realm would recognize him.

Once we have become someone recognized by the dharma realm, what have we to worry about? What should we fight tooth and nail to possess? Let us all practice with diligence so that each of us becomes a person recognized by the dharma realm and the wielder of that awesome power.

## "...and be unified with the substance and nature of Il-Won."

Unification with the substance and nature of Il-Won means that we awaken to the Dharmakāya Buddha Il-Won-Sang Truth that governs and is ever with all the myriad things of the universe and the dharma-realm of empty space, and that we live like that truth. There is but one Il-Won-Sang Truth in this universe. It is not the case that God, Heaven, and the Way exist separately; there is only the one truth. The one truth is called "the pure Dharmakāya Buddha."

When we see the nature and experience the great enlightenment of the Dharmakāya Buddha and model our body and mind wholeheartedly on its purity, this is called "the perfect Sambhogakāya Buddha." When we have experienced and come to possess the truth as it is in this way, we are said to have become a buddha.

When those who have become Sambhogakāya Buddhas interact with sentient beings, their wisdom and mercy linger within the sentient beings' mind as the Nirāmaṇakāya Buddha. This means something has become deeply impressed as a standard for faith in the Buddha and for our own character. When we possess this triple Buddha body in one person, it is said that we have become unified with the substance and nature of the Il-Won-Sang Truth.

The beginning part of the vow says that the Il-Won is "the realm of samādhi beyond all words and speech." This means existing in a state of samādhi in every place and time. The vow also says that the Il-Won is "the gateway of birth and death that transcends being and nonbeing." When we are capable of generating and collecting minds from a position that transcends all things, we can say that we have become unified with the substance and nature.

"The Dharma of Timeless Sŏn" tells us that we must learn the Way through practice that takes true voidness as the substance and marvelous existence as the function. When we learn the Way maturely so that we never part with our self-nature, this is unification with the substance and nature. The Founding Master said that we must file a registration transfer to complete a deed transferring the dharma realm of empty space into our own possession. In other words, we must make the void-like thing that is the truth into something that is utterly ours.

When we buy or sell property, we typically pay an escrow deposit, intermediate payment, and the balance, and then we go to the registration office and complete a deed transfer. Only when we have the deed in our name does something become completely our property. In the same way, transferring the deed of the Il-Won-Sang Truth into our name requires the investment of tremendous amounts of mind, body, and matter. When we want to start a business, we must invest money, time, and passion.

Of course, there is a bit of difference when investing in awakening to and uniting with the Il-Won-Sang Truth, but I believe the difference is trivial in terms of their requiring an investment. When we are investing in a business, we should also be investing in making the Il-Won-Sang ours. That way, both ventures can prosper all the more.

When we speak of modeling ourselves wholeheartedly on the Il-Won-Sang Truth, this means emulation, but a person cannot emulate anything if that person has not discovered a model worthy of emulation. What should the person do? That person should listen to the experience of others who have already modeled themselves on the Il-Won-Sang in their practice, and act according to that experience. This is what leads us to place our faith in teachers and study the scriptures, which are an account of this experience.

We must maintain faith in teachers for a long time and diligently do as they instruct. As we do so, we will discover the footprints of the truth.

"Seeing the nature" means the discovery of a mind that is the realm of the great, the realm of voidness, and the realm of nonbeing. When we have done so, we will have awakened to our own ever-calm and ever-alert mind. This mind—the realm of the great, the realm of voidness, and the realm of nonbeing—is called the truth that neither arises nor ceases. Awakening to this means understanding the jewel that lies within us.

We must recognize this and make tremendous investments so that we can register it in our name. We must commit ourselves sincerely—investing our devotion, investing our time, and sometimes investing pure wealth—so that we may awaken to the "no mind."

Once we engage in mind-practice in more depth, we will awaken to the fact that the truth of retribution and response of cause and effect, in which we reap as we sow, is not at all separate from the principle of alternating predominance of *yin* and *yang* that accounts for changes in the universe, and we will also awaken to the fact that actions that are right and wrong, beneficial and harmful, are not separate from the principles of great and small, being and nonbeing. We will awaken with certitude to the fact that the principles of the mind are the actions of the universe. This is called the "Perfect and Right Enlightenment."

Based on this awakening to all principles and understanding of all affairs, we will go on to exert ourselves. We must engage in sincere and great exertion so that we attain the status of beyond the household and the status of greatly enlightened tathāgata. At that time, we will become unified with the *ātman* of the universe. At that time, we will enter the samādhi state of one suchness in action and rest, where action and rest are one. In the *Diamond Sutra*, this is called "nirvana without remainder." It is a state of unbroken nirvana, of ultimate bliss in every time and place.

The Founding Master said that the sentient being suffers because its mind does not operate as the being wishes, creating a hell within the mind; that the sentient being's body becomes accustomed to function as it will because the being does not know its body well enough, creating an agonizing hell; and that because the sentient being does not know how to use its mind to deal with its affinities and relationships, it creates a hell within those affinities.

The life of the bodhisattva, however, is one in which we know the principles of our mind and train it accordingly; we know our body and train our body and habits effectively; and we approach our affinities with the dharma mind—turning the mind, the body, our affinities, the world, heaven, and earth into ultimate bliss, and becoming the masters of bliss ourselves.

This truly is unification with the substance and nature of the Il-Won-Sang Truth.

# Chapter Eight

# CONCLUSION OF THE IL-WON-SANG VOW

We must live lives according to a will. We must have the will to become buddhas and benefit the world; we should not live for pleasure. If we live for pleasure and enjoyment, we may enjoy ourselves for a time, but we will not know what to do later when we encounter pain.

There is a genuine pleasure that arises when we live according to a will. This is not just any ordinary will, however; all of us must adopt the truth as our home, adopt the actions of the truth as our actions, defeat Māra and bring it into submission. We must have a firm vow to progress and receive great grace. It is important to know whether we have that will or not at this moment.

If we make a certain vow here and now, in the realm of the

gods they will hold an early consecration ceremony for us. "That person is sure to be a buddha before long," they will say. "Let's hold the consecration now."

The gist of the vow could be described as an instruction to "live according to a will," to "live based on the will to become a buddha."

How many times do you recite the Il-Won-Sang Vow each day? If you do it ten times a day or more, then you are doing around five thousand recitations in a year. Some people are said to recite it twenty times in the morning and evening. For those of you who do so, I ask that you do it without thinking of the will for a time, and then do it one or two times while pondering the will.

As for those who have not yet done it, I ask that you do ten to twenty recitations each day. If you recite it frequently, the grace of the sages will be with you. Those in the divine realm are not careless with the person who has frequently recited the scriptures of the Buddha.

There are a number of things that the Founding Master said very frequently. I will tell you about one of them.

There was a Confucian scholar named Lee. One day it was raining heavily and he entered a temple to escape the downpour. Next to the temple, he saw written the words "The Flower Ornament Sutra." That's a good name for a sutra, he thought to himself.

Some time after that, he was killed as he was about to enter a nice house by someone who suddenly struck his head with a wooden clapper and said, "Hey! What is a guy who learned the *Flower Ornament Sutra* heading for a doghouse?" At this, the scholar is said to have revived with a start.

Those who recite the Buddha's teachings frequently are said to be assisted by the good gods and good asuras that exist to help the Buddha. They help the Buddha by guiding the person who has recited his teachings frequently onto the proper path. They ask, "Is it right that such a person should end up in a doghouse?"

If we work constantly toward the ten thousand cultivations, inquiries, and cultivations of virtue, the billion cultivations, inquiries, and cultivations of virtue, and the immeasurable cultivations, inquiries, and cultivations of virtue, we will change the nameplate on our door. We will no longer be the sentient beings that we were before. Our plate will read "buddha-bodhisattva" instead.

Until that day, I hope that every one of you will perform the great exertion.

This book on the Il-Won-Sang Vow has been compiled from recordings of lectures given over a nine-day period at the Tuesday retreat during my time as Executive Director of Seoul Regional. The lectures were delivered so that *Won*-Buddhists and I might inherit and practice the Founding Master's plan for mercy, and they are seeing publication only now, several years later.

At times, the lectures want for systematic explanation, and at times I pass things over if I believe they indicate a situation that everyone already understands. As such, there are some areas in the book that are lacking in systematicity and explanation. For this reason, I have reviewed the text and added some information, but because it is structured around lecture content there are some aspects that I find unsatisfactory in its publication as a book. Still, I decided to publish it anyway, hoping that it would serve as an opportunity to understand the great teacher's will in some small degree. If the reader notifies me of any aspect of it that is wanting, I will humbly accept the suggestions and revise it accordingly.

I would like to extend my sincerest appreciation to the *kyomu* who worked hard to make the recordings and provide revisions and supplementation for the publication of this book, and to all of the *kyomu* who published it.

– The Author

## Credits

Author      Prime Dharma Master Kyongsan
Translator   Colin Mouat

Publisher   Kim Hyung-geun
Editor      Kim Eugene
Designer   Lee Bok-hyun